Student Writing in the Quantitative Disciplines

TCC South

Crowley Learning Center

Student Writing in the Quantitative Disciplines

A GUIDE FOR COLLEGE FACULTY

Patrick Bahls

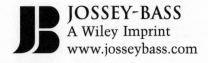

JOSSEY-BASS
A Wiley Imprint
www.josseybass.com

Published by Jossey-Bass
A Wiley Imprint
One Montgomery Street, Suite 1200, San Francisco, CA 94104-4594—www.josseybass.com

Jossey-Bass books and products are available through most bookstores. To contact Jossey-Bass directly call our Customer Care Department within the U.S. at 800-956-7739, outside the U.S. at 317-572-3986, or fax 317-572-4002.

Wiley also publishes its books in a variety of electronic formats and by print-on-demand. Some material included with standard print versions of this book may not be included in e-books or in print-on-demand. If the version of this book that you purchased references media such as CD or DVD that was not included in your purchase, you may download this material at http://booksupport.wiley.com. For more information about Wiley products, visit www.wiley.com.

Library of Congress Cataloging-in-Publication Data

Bahls, Patrick, 1975-
    Student writing in the quantitative disciplines : a guide for college faculty / Patrick Bahls. — 1st ed.
        p.   cm. — (The Jossey-Bass higher and adult education series)
    Includes bibliographical references and index.
    ISBN 978-0-470-95212-2 (pbk.); ISBN 978-1-118-20580-8 (ebk.)
    ISBN 978-1-118-20581-5 (ebk.); ISBN 978-1-118-20582-2 (ebk.)
        1. Mathematics—Authorship.   2. Mathematics—Study and teaching (Higher)   I. Title.
    QA20.M38B34   2012
    808.06'651—dc23

                                                                    2011046150

Printed in the United States of America
FIRST EDITION
PB Printing   10 9 8 7 6 5 4 3 2 1

The Jossey-Bass Higher and
Adult Education Series

To Maggie

CONTENTS

PREFACE

"I got into math because I don't like to write!"

Do your students say this whenever you ask them to write more than a few simple lines of computation? Do they revolt when you encourage them to contextualize their computations or to justify them or explain them in qualitative terms? Do they insist that it doesn't really matter how they got to the right answer, as long as they got there in the end, so it makes no difference that they can't explain their reasoning once they are done?

I write this book for college faculty in mathematics, statistics, physics, engineering, economics, chemistry, computer science . . . in any subject, really, in which quantitative reasoning is central and in which writing has traditionally played a secondary role. I write this book to help faculty in these quantitative disciplines see how writing figures prominently in the learning process and to learn how to more meaningfully incorporate writing into even the most purely mathematical of college courses. I write this book to help these faculty enable their students not only to become better writers in their disciplines but also to use writing as a tool for learning and for examining and analyzing new ideas.

I write as an instructor who deals daily with students' resistance to writing. Not a semester goes by without a handful of the first-year college students in my calculus classes declaring their distaste for writing, generally midway through the course's first major writing assignment. They say it honestly, and without malice or guilt. They say it like I should take pity on them and knowing how they feel excuse them from writing for the rest of the semester. Students enter their math classes expecting to write very little, if at all. For most of them, math courses focus on formulas and computations. Math to them is numbers, a smattering of symbols, some assorted "thuses" and "therefores," and that's exactly how students like it. Few students have ever been asked to write in complete sentences in their math classes, and from their perspective this is a good thing. As a consequence, students don't recognize what writing in mathematics looks like, in part because many of us have a hard time describing it, let alone explaining why it is important.

Nevertheless, writing has a place in every course, even in courses with quantitative content, in which numbers typically take center stage. Even in math, well-structured writing assignments help students learn how to communicate clearly what they have learned. Even in disciplines like math, statistics, physics, engineering, economics, chemistry, and computer science, reflective writing helps students focus on the learning experience itself. Writing helps students in these areas organize and clarify their thoughts. It helps them discover others' ideas and develop their own. It helps them gain a sense of authorship and take charge of their own learning.

This book is written for instructors in any discipline that offers courses with heavy quantitative content, courses in which students regularly make claims like "I got into this major because I don't like to write" or "I won't need to write much for what I plan to do." This book will help you respond to these claims by showing students what a powerful learning tool writing can be, in any field. The following chapters answer many of the questions you may have regarding the role of writing in quantitative disciplines:

- How can writing help me meet my course learning goals?
- How can I convince my students that writing is worthwhile?
- How can I design assignments that will help my students become better writers?
- How can I respond to the writing my students create for these assignments?
- Where can I go to learn more about writing and how to teach it?
- How can I do all of the above without adding hours to the time it takes me to prepare for class?

This last question is a crucial one. Rest assured that I include a number of strategies to help you incorporate writing into your courses in ways that are both effective and efficient. Indeed, some simple writing activities take only a minute or two of class time for your students to complete them, and no more than ten or twelve minutes outside of class for you to respond. Lengthier assignments, naturally, take more time both for you and for your students, but there are ways of making even the most involved projects more manageable and worth the time they take.

Your students will have questions and concerns of their own, and this book will help you respond to them confidently:

- Why do I have to write in this class? Aren't I just supposed to find the right answer?

- You're not an English teacher. What do you know about teaching writing?

- I'm not used to writing like this. What am I supposed to say in this paper?

- I'm not here to learn writing. I'm here to solve problems.

This last objection is one of the hardest to address, particularly because many of us find it easy to sympathize with the students who voice it. Our disciplines are very content oriented, and many of us struggle to find the time to teach our students everything our syllabi say we are supposed to. Given all of the content we have to cover, when can we find time to help our students with their writing? How can we make sure that even while we're helping students become better writers, we're still helping them master disciplinary ideas?

It is clear that time spent on writing is time not spent on something else. If over the course of a semester you take two or three hours of class time for writing instruction, peer review, or other writing-related activities, you take two or three hours of class time away from direct treatment of course content. Particularly in highly regimented lower-level courses, this might mean you will have to consider a few sections of material with less depth than you would have otherwise or that you will have to skip one or two sections altogether.

However, as I hope to show you in this book, writing in the disciplines is worth a few hours' sacrifice, and in fact writing need not distract your students from learning the content of your course. To the contrary, effective writing assignments will help your students contextualize course content as they assemble disparate ideas from your discipline and discover new ideas of their own. These assignments will assist your students in answering the questions "How?"

and "Why?" rather than simply "What?" Put another way, writing and written assignments do not replace the content with which courses in the quantitative disciplines are concerned; rather, they complement that content and give it context and richness. Seen in this way, writing is not so much an end but a means. It is a lens through which course content can be viewed, giving that content greater depth and clarity.

A WRITING AUTOBIOGRAPHY

I begin by saying a bit about my own experience with incorporating writing in my math courses. The following brief history points out some of the missteps I've made and the pitfalls I've fallen into as I have learned more about teaching students to write in my own discipline. Because the rest of this book offers a variety of ways to avoid those, I say little about that here. The message I'd most like you to take from this history is that learning to teach writing takes time. You can't expect to do it perfectly right away.

My attempts at including writing in my mathematics courses began several years ago in graduate school. My early efforts to involve writing in these courses were clumsy. As these efforts became more focused and purposeful, I became acutely aware of the need for a more comprehensive treatment of both the theory and practice of writing in the quantitative disciplines. In the following pages I offer an overview of the journey I have taken, and an outline for this book, which in many ways is a record of that journey.

Why Use Writing in the Mathematics Classroom? . . . Why Not?

In the fall of 1999 I began my second year of graduate school at Vanderbilt University. Before that I had been a teaching assistant with limited course duties, but in fall 1999 I was given full responsibility for the design and delivery of a first-semester course in calculus. I felt I was ready for the job. I had spent the past few years developing a number of teaching techniques I hoped to put to work in my courses, and I'd finally been given a chance to use them. I was excited to find out how well they would work.

Among those techniques was the use of writing. As a person who's always used writing to organize my thoughts, I knew there had to be a place for writing in the mathematics classroom. I'm embarrassed to admit that with no formal training in writing instruction, this was about *all* that I knew about teaching writing. I was naïve, but I earnestly wanted to succeed.

My first writing assignment, given roughly halfway into that first calculus course, was a simple one: "Select a mathematical topic of interest to you and write a five- to ten-page paper about it." I gave my students minimal direction and few format restrictions, as I thought that this would free them to be creative. I asked for no rough drafts, as I had only rarely been asked for such drafts when I had written papers as an undergraduate. I assumed that my students had come to my class as fully formed writers who needed no further guidance. If they were strong writers they would write well, and if they were weak writers they would write poorly.

The students did most of their work on their own and only rarely consulted with me. Near the end of the term I collected their papers. Having given the students nearly half of the semester to complete what I thought was a rather short and straightforward assignment, I was stunned by the quality of their papers. Their writing was unfocused and riddled with grammatical, syntactical, and logical errors. The weakest papers were nearly unreadable and the strongest were rigid and formulaic. I know now that the former could have been improved dramatically had the students been asked to redraft their work at least once, and the latter had I held a short in-class discussion on style and tone. All of the students would have benefited from a clearer prompt that asked them to write for a particular audience.

I know now that my earliest attempt at incorporating writing could serve well as a list of writing-in-the-discipline "don'ts":

- Don't assume students will understand, or even recognize, the audience for whom they are to write.

- Don't assume that students understand how to write in a particular genre without some explanation, however brief, of the conventions of that genre.

- Don't assume that students will produce finely crafted papers in response to a poorly or vaguely worded prompt.

- Don't assume that students will produce finely crafted papers without a properly staged assignment that includes multiple drafts and opportunities for feedback.

- Don't respond slavishly to students' grammatical and syntactical mistakes.

Clearly I had a lot to learn about teaching writing.

As awkward as my first attempts at including writing were, I persisted, and over the next few years my efforts at weaving writing into my courses improved significantly. I kept that same assignment for a while, tweaking it, elaborating on the prompt, and providing more direction. At some point I added the requirement that students submit a rough draft. The students' writing, on average, got better, and this encouraged me to include simpler, smaller writing assignments in my classes, including some I now recognize as what the literature calls *writing-to-learn* activities. (I describe that term more fully later in this book.)

My students' writing continued to improve, and I started to notice other benefits. The writing seemed to help the students become more engaged, and it helped them gain a better conceptual understanding of the computations they were performing. Writing helped them go from knowing *how* to apply a particular formula to knowing *why* they were applying it. These benefits convinced me that even though writing took a little bit of time away from traditional treatment of the course's content, the time students spent on writing was time well spent indeed.

This benefit was even evident in the feedback I got from my students on the writing I asked them to do. Judging from the comments I was getting on midterm evaluations, it was clear I was doing something right:

- "That exercise really helped me understand what was going on with derivatives."
- "The writing was a nice break from all the formulas we were studying for the past three weeks."
- "It really helped me when we wrote about the work we did in class the past few days."
- "Writing the proofs made sense, but they made even more sense when I had to write about the writing I was doing."

Comments like these encouraged me to continue using writing in my courses and to learn about new ways to use it.

The Next Steps

During the summer after my first year at the University of North Carolina Asheville, I took part in two faculty development activities that had a profound effect on my teaching of writing.

The first of these activities was a two-day workshop organized by the university's Writing Intensive Committee and centered on Katherine K. Gottschalk and Keith Hjortshoj's slender but substantial book, *The Elements of Teaching Writing: A Resource for Instructors in All Disciplines* (2004). One of the goals of the workshop was to convince faculty who were on the fence that writing has a valuable role in every course, in every discipline. Another goal was to provide faculty who were interested in designing a writing-intensive course with the basic skills they would need to put such a course together. The workshop's leaders, faculty from our institution, taught participating faculty how writing could be used to accomplish course goals and about the ways writing could be incorporated meaningfully into just about any classroom. I finished this workshop feeling energized, with several fresh ideas for using writing in my own courses, some of which I describe in Chapters Four and Five.

The second activity was a faculty learning circle sponsored by the university's Center for Teaching and Learning and based on L. Dee Fink's text *Creating Significant Learning Experiences: An Integrated Approach to Designing College Courses* (2003). This book is replete with inventive strategies for engaging students and empowering them to take control of their own learning. Writing figures prominently in many of those strategies. Reading Fink's text and discussing it with my colleagues in the learning circle helped me to see that writing isn't just a superficial supplement to any given course. Rather, I began to see how writing can help students engage course content on a deeper level, even in courses far removed from traditionally writing-intensive areas. I began to see how writing could be integrated with other learning activities. The learning circle motivated me to apply for writing-intensive status for the linear algebra course I would be teaching in fall 2006.

In order to meet to my school's expectations for writing-intensive courses, I made sure to include a number of writing activities that would challenge my students both to write authentically in their discipline and to write reflectively about the experiences they had as they worked to master the content in the course. Students would spend the semester working on successively more robust drafts of a traditional research paper. They would also respond to a wide variety of "low-stakes" writing assignments, including three-minute microthemes, learning logs, and collaborative conceptual quizzes.

The first time through, I still made some mistakes. I know now that with a bit more preparation I could have saved myself a great deal of effort. For instance, had I put in place some system of peer review, I could have avoided offering feedback on every one of the several drafts of the students' research papers. Had I known it was pedagogically permissible to do so, I could have responded only occasionally to each student's learning log entries, saving myself an hour or two of reading and responding every week. Most important, had I thought the matter through I would have realized that any one of the several new activities I had introduced would have been beneficial, and that I need not have added them all at once. I know now that, like any curricular changes, changes in the role of writing in a given course are best made incrementally, a little bit at a time. After all, it is better to make a few thoughtful adjustments carefully than to implement sweeping changes haphazardly.

My steps were shaky ones, but I made fewer missteps than I had in the past, and the quality of the writing my students crafted was uniformly high. Moreover, I sensed that students had gained greater understanding of the concepts of the course due to my request that they write reflectively about them. Even though teaching the class left me exhausted, helping my students learn to write in their discipline was one of the most rewarding teaching experiences I have yet had. Moreover, I had discovered an unexpected benefit of incorporating writing in my classes: the writing assignments I had introduced were as new to me as they were to my students, and they offered me a way to reinvigorate my teaching. By giving me fresh ways of approaching the material I'd taught several times before, writing helped me to get over my boredom of discussing determinants *yet again*. Writing forced me to reinvent the way I'd been teaching for the past several years, and this reinvention was challenging, intriguing, and fun.

In the following semesters I began creating more writing assignments for students in all of my courses. I write about all of these activities, and many others designed by instructors in a broad variety of quantitative disciplines in later chapters, but I offer some brief highlights here:

- Students in my Calculus I courses produce a variety of documents pertaining to the mock trial between Isaac Newton and Gottfried Leibniz that they stage in class.

- Students in my precalculus courses write poems with some sort of mathematical structure, content, or theme. They have a chance to share these with one another in a reading near the semester's end.

- Students in all of my upper-level courses serve on "homework committees" tasked with performing peer reviews of drafts of homework solutions. They write reports summarizing their reviews in which they highlight frequent mistakes and uncommon insights.

- Students in all of my courses craft dialogues in which they explain advanced mathematical concepts to a fictional peer who struggles valiantly, but seemingly endlessly, with each course's content.

- Students in my course on mathematical proofs write frequently about writing as they analyze the subtle meaning of various mathematical terms and phrases.

- Students in this same course spend the semester collaborating on a "textbook" for the course. The students in one semester's class wrote a seventy-page booklet and spoke about their experience in writing it at a regional mathematics conference.

A few of these activities I invented myself, and many others I adapted from assignments I had read about or heard about from colleagues in other disciplines. Indeed, as I grew more serious about incorporating writing in my courses, I began a thorough search for more and better ways to do this.

Reading Up

The ideas I found came from many places, not just my own discipline. I took a position on my university's Writing Intensive Committee, which gave me the opportunity to borrow ideas my colleagues in other departments had dreamed up. I also read widely on teaching writing, uncovering in my search everything from general texts on writing instruction to sourcebooks containing sample prompts and writing assignment outlines. I attended sessions on writing at mathematics conferences, and I attended sessions for faculty in math and sciences at conferences for scholars of writing and composition.

Although I have learned a great deal from this research, I have also come to realize that there are holes in the existing literature on writing in quantitative disciplines. There are useful relevant sources, but most of them focus on one or another aspect of writing in quantitative fields to the neglect of other aspects. None of them provides a comprehensive background in both the theory and practice of writing in quantitative areas. This background would benefit instructors in these areas who are interested in incorporating more writing in their courses.

Many sources, generally written by instructors in quantitative disciplines, offer concrete and practical support to the aspiring teacher of writing in the form of writing activities, assignments, and exercises. In pedagogical periodicals, and indeed in some books, I have discovered many examples of writing assignments that can be used in quantitative courses, but they are offered without the information instructors need to use them successfully. (See, for instance, Crannell, LaRose,

Ratliff, & Rykken, 2004, or Meier & Rishel, 1998.) In a way these publications are like cookbooks: they offer many delicious recipes for the experienced cook, but should the reader not know how to turn on the stove, the recipes are nothing more than pretty pictures on the page. The assignments can be creative and effective teaching tools, but the sources they're found in often fail to give the teacher the assistance she needs to structure the assignments properly, to respond to the writing the students produce for the assignments, or to assess the quality of that writing. The collections of such articles that gather together a number of assignments in one place offer similarly little instructional context. Most of these sources simply seem to assume that our students learn to write "somewhere else" and that they carry their writing skills, fully formed, into our quantitative courses.

Other sources, generally written by experts in composition or writing instruction, err in the opposite direction. While they give teachers a robust introduction to the ideas of writing in the disciplines and cover topics like assignment design, assessment, and responding meaningfully to student writing, most of these sources give only a handful of such examples, if any at all, for instructors in quantitative disciplines. Sometimes one or two assignments are meant to serve as illustrations for all related disciplines, as if writing in mathematics differed little from writing in computer science or in engineering or in mathematical finance. The authors of these sources often simply avoid dealing with the idiosyncrasies of writing in math-based fields. To extend the cooking metaphor, these sources are like how-to manuals that tell the vegetarian everything she needs to know about preparing succulent beef-based dishes with the hope that the culinary skills developed in one kitchen will carry over into a very different one.

Here we assemble a more complete menu by putting together all the ingredients and following every recipe, step by step, from turning on the oven to garnishing the last delectable dish . . . and deciding whether or not that dish should ever be served again. Every step is crucial, and I hope that this book will give you the skills and the confidence you will need to perform each one well.

In order to guide our students in authentic and purposeful writing activities, we must understand the underlying principles of writing in the disciplines and writing-to-learn. We must also give ourselves a wide variety of creative writing assignments appropriate to our fields. Finally, we must have confidence that not only are we qualified to teach writing in our respective disciplines, but moreover *no one else* is better qualified than we are.

LEARNING TO COOK, ONE DISH AT A TIME

In Chapter One, I give a brief introduction to writing across the curriculum, writing in the disciplines, and writing-to-learn. *Writing across the curriculum* refers to the idea that writing is an activity that takes place in every class, not just in English or composition courses. Therefore the responsibility for teaching writing falls upon every instructor, regardless of her academic background. *Writing in the disciplines* refers to the idea that students should be given opportunities to write authentically in their own fields of study, and that instructors in those disciplines are the best instructors of such writing. Finally, *writing-to-learn* refers to the use of writing, often ungraded or "low-stakes" writing, whose primary purpose is to help students both to learn and to reflect on their learning. In the first chapter I define these terms more carefully and sketch the growth of their interrelated movements. More important, I describe what writing in the disciplines and writing-to-learn look like in quantitative fields. Finally, I address some of the challenges you will face in writing in the disciplines and writing-to-learn, and I mention some of the rewards you will receive for taking time to involve writing so meaningfully.

The next couple of chapters will help you get a handle on the writing process and on assessing and responding to student writing. Though I occasionally indicate some of the theoretical principles underlying writing in the disciplines, my primary goal in these chapters is to provide you with practical ways of making writing work in your courses. Chapter Two offers an overview of the process underlying academic writing, a process that involves prewriting, organizing, drafting, review, and revision. The notion of writing as a process is particularly important to those of us who teach in the quantitative disciplines, as our students are often concerned solely with the finished product of their computations and not the nature of those computations themselves. If students are helped to see how each step in the writing process enables them to make their ideas clearer, more complete, and more correct, they are more likely to engage in this process.

In Chapter Three, I address writing assessment and responding to students' writing. This issue is a particularly puzzling one in quantitative disciplines: How can we judge the quality of the mathematical writing our students produce? To what extent does *correctness* play a role in assessment, given its centrality in quantitative fields? How can we respond to students' writing in order to best offer them means to improve their writing? Although every assignment is different and no set of guidelines will apply equally well in every setting, we develop some general criteria for the assessment of students' writing in quantitative fields. Furthermore, I give some tips on giving feedback to students in writing and face-to-face conferencing, and I offer advice on preparing students to perform peer reviews of each others' work.

In Chapters Four and Five, I serve up a cornucopia of writing assignments and activities. The first of these chapters focuses on informal and low-stakes writing activities, while the second treats more formal and highly structured assignments. Most of these activities will be suitable, appropriately modified, for use in a broad variety of quantitative courses. I draw on the wealth of existing sources that offer descriptions of such activities and give the reader a number of references for further reading. I supplement these sources with a large number of activities I've found helpful in my own classrooms. With every activity I include guidelines for structuring the activity, responding to students' writing, and assessing their work when appropriate. My hope is that after reading these chapters you will be able to help your students understand how writing can be a useful tool both for *communicating* the content of their courses and for *learning* that content in the first place.

In Chapter Six I bring the book to a close with a brief discussion of the roles those who teach writing in quantitative disciplines should assume. First and foremost, the instructor should be an effective *teacher* of writing, careful to provide students with the skills they will need both to write well in their fields and to use writing as a tool for lifelong disciplinary learning. To do this most effectively, the instructor should also be a *scholar* of writing in the disciplines. She should be willing to stay abreast of new ideas on using writing in quantitative courses and to share what she has learned about teaching writing with others. Finally, the instructor should be a *champion* for writing in the disciplines, reaching out to her colleagues in the field who need to be persuaded to include writing in their own courses and to her colleagues in writing with whom her knowledge can be shared.

FOR WHOM DO I WRITE?

As I mentioned at the start of this Preface, first and foremost I am writing for my colleagues in the quantitative disciplines. I use the general term *quantitative disciplines* in order to reach not only those who teach in mathematics and in the disciplines typically included under the heading "mathematical sciences" (physics, engineering, and computer science, for example), but also those who teach in less traditionally mathematical areas that involve a substantial amount of quantitative or numerical content. Certain courses in chemistry, biology, and economics certainly fit this description, as do courses in statistics and quantitative methods intended for students of psychology, sociology, education, and other social sciences.

Incorporating writing into classes in these fields has not been addressed as thoroughly as it needs to be. This book fills gaps in current discussions of writing instruction in these areas. Faculty in the quantitative disciplines who are new to teaching writing will gain a great deal from reading the book from the start. In particular, I believe this book will serve as a useful complement to the style guides and technical manuals that lay out expectations for writing in specific disciplines. While these manuals may do a great job of describing the genres in which practitioners of respective disciplines write, they often do little to describe how students can be taught to write in those genres.

Furthermore, I believe that instructors who are already familiar with writing instruction can learn much from this book. They will glean some time-saving tips on responding to and assessing student writing from Chapters Two and Three and some useful ideas for writing exercises from Chapters Four and Five. Given the quantitative disciplines' peripheral position in rhetoric and composition, I am certain that experts in writing (especially instructors in first-year composition courses and writing center staff) will benefit from these examples as well.

I should admit at the outset that though this book offers a more comprehensive treatment of writing instruction in the math-based disciplines than has been offered before, the book does not treat the subject exhaustively. Though fields like computer science, mechanical engineering, mathematical finance, and biostatistics all share a common quantitative base, they differ from one another in many substantive ways that no single book can address. What I offer here marks a starting point from which the role of writing in our fields and in our courses can be explored more fully.

However you choose to read this book, I hope in reading it you will become more confident in identifying realistic disciplinary learning outcomes related to and accessible through writing, in designing written assignments to help your students achieve those outcomes, and in responding meaningfully to your students' written work.

ACKNOWLEDGMENTS

I am tremendously grateful to many people without whose help and support this book would not have been possible.

I owe thanks to my wonderful colleagues at the University of North Carolina Asheville for their continual support and encouragement. A few people deserve special mention. Karin Peterson merits such mention for giving me inspiration early in my study of writing, and Katherine Min has earned her place here by offering her helpful reader responses to my writing. And then there are my fellow mathematicians, Sam Kaplan and Janine Haugh: both are sources of numerous fantastic teaching ideas, and neither can resist taking a good idea and making it better. To them I owe thanks for helping me think through all of my teaching practices, including those involving writing.

I owe thanks also to my many friends in the Carolinas Writing Program Administrators. I am grateful not just for their insights on writing and writing instruction but moreover for bringing me into a warm and welcoming community of lifelong learners. Among these people, special thanks are due to Kerri Flinchbaugh, for helping me to untangle early drafts of several chapters, and Mary Alm, for being among the first to introduce me to writing across the curriculum.

I am in no way less grateful to my students, whose tirelessness and dedication often fill me with awe and admiration. They've been open-minded enough to try to new things and honest enough to let me know when those new things need adjustment to make them work properly. I am particularly grateful to those students who have let me include their work in this book.

Thanks are due also to the staff at Jossey-Bass, including David Brightman and Aneesa Davenport, for their prompt attention to my many queries, and to my consulting editor, Maryellen Weimer, who always seemed able to hear what I was trying to say, even when I wasn't sure I was trying to say it. Her fast and forthright feedback helped me make the most of every word.

I cannot close without mentioning my wonderful wife, Maggie Hoop, the first reader for nearly everything I write. I thank her for patiently accepting the hundreds of hours this book took away from the time we might have otherwise spent together.

ABOUT THE AUTHOR

Patrick Bahls studied mathematics at the University of Denver and Vanderbilt University, earning his doctoral degree at Vanderbilt in 2002. After teaching at Vanderbilt and the University of Illinois, he moved to the University of North Carolina (UNC) Asheville, where he is now an associate professor in the mathematics department. Writing has always played a central role in his classes, in which students complete a number of activities designed both to help them learn to master the conventions of mathematical writing and to assist their learning of mathematical ideas. Bahls served on UNC Asheville's committee on writing-intensive courses for four years and is now a member of its committee on first-year writing. He has presented on issues related to writing across the curriculum, writing in the disciplines, and writing-to-learn at several regional, national, and international conferences, including the annual meeting of the Carolinas Writing Program Administrators and the biannual International Writing Across the Curriculum Conference.

Understanding the Role of Writing

Ass I admitted in the Preface, my own route to writing in the math classroom was a rocky one. I did no research on writing and had few models for writing assignments before I began assigning writing projects to my students. In fact, several years would pass before it came to me that perhaps I ought to see what writing scholars had to say about designing discipline-specific writing activities. Much of what I learned about writing I picked up through experimentation, and I often felt I was alone in my belief that writing could play a pivotal part in students' learning of math.

I know now that I was never alone. In fact, one of the first things I learned when I read about what others had done was that I was a newcomer to a movement that had started many years before. There is a long tradition of disciplinary writing and disciplinary writing instruction to which scholars in every academic field have contributed. These contributions continue and have helped the writing across the curriculum movement grow into a force that has changed what students experience in many classrooms across our campuses.

My goal in this first chapter is to offer an introduction to this movement, to its past, and to its possibilities. Our first step is to define the key terms that are used frequently throughout this book, namely *writing across the curriculum*, *writing in the disciplines*, and *writing-to-learn*. None of these terms has fixed definitions: their meanings are flexible, broad, and subject to interpretation.

Moreover, the boundaries among them are blurry. For instance, the collection of courses some institutions would call a "WAC [writing across the curriculum] program" others would just as quickly call a "WID [writing in the disciplines] program." In fact, for many purposes the latter two terms can be used to refer to components of the former, as if writing in the disciplines and writing-to-learn are simply ways in which writing across the curriculum manifests itself. From this point of view, "writing in the disciplines" refers to faculty efforts to teach students to write as authentic practitioners of the fields they study. Meanwhile, "writing-to-learn" refers to writing that is more than a means of communicating ideas; this writing can be used to generate ideas and to understand those ideas better by helping the writer think critically about them. Particularly relevant to those of us working in problem-based quantitative fields, this kind of writing helps the writer hone problem-solving skills.

I then spend a few pages laying out a brief history of the writing across the curriculum movement, leaving a fuller treatment to references like Russell (1994). My hope is that this historical context will show you how writing has found a home in a wide variety of disciplinary courses. I indicate some of the forms writing may take in the quantitative disciplines. These forms are anything but clear, and we face certain obstacles when we attempt to adapt writing strategies to quantitative courses. The most difficult of these obstacles to overcome is the resistance that students (and sometimes, sadly, instructors!) often show to writing. I end the chapter by examining both the sources of this resistance and the ways we can overcome it.

BASIC DEFINITIONS

The term *writing across the curriculum* (WAC) refers to the recognition that neither academic writing nor academic writing instruction can be confined to a single department or collection of courses. Nor can it be relegated to one or two semesters of "composition" in a student's first year of study. Rather, students of every discipline must be exposed to writing activities of their courses at every level. This exposure is essential if students are to develop the writing skills they'll need to write in a wide variety of genres and for diverse audiences. After all, the most important writing students will do will take place after graduation, when they find themselves in professions that require strong communication skills for success.

Writing in the disciplines (WID) refers to discipline-specific writing activities designed to give students experience in writing according to the conventions of a given discipline. Only by exercising these conventions regularly and completing realistic writing tasks, often called "authentic" assignments, will students grow accustomed to the sort of writing they will be expected to do as practitioners of their disciplines. Clearly, the persons most qualified to direct students' development as disciplinary writers are scholars of those disciplines. Thus writing instruction is the responsibility of every instructor, in every discipline.

The writing we do in quantitative fields serves many purposes. Much of our public writing communicates our ideas to one another, in academic articles, technical reports, or conference proceedings. However, a great deal of disciplinary writing is less formal, less structured, and remains unpublished. We write emails to our colleagues and memos to ourselves. We scribble formulas and figures in the margins of our textbooks as we wrestle with others' ideas, and we make outlines, lists, and diagrams as we come up with new ideas of our own. All of these informal forms of writing serve to help us think and learn, and therefore are called *writing-to-learn* (WTL). Often WTL activities are referred to as "low-stakes writing" to reinforce the notion that these activities are informal and that, though they are certainly not inconsequential exercises, they should not be treated as opportunities to grade students on their writing.

It's hard to make a clear distinction between WID and WTL. The writing done by scholars in any discipline will involve elements of both. For instance, WTL methods often underlie the composition of more complicated disciplinary writing most would place under the WID heading. Few of us would dream of drafting a journal article without first producing page after page of exploratory scratchwork. WAC, WID, and WTL are overlapping, interdependent, and otherwise closely related.

The histories of these ideas are as difficult to disentangle from one another as are the ideas themselves. It would be hard, if not impossible, to place a pin at the point at which the WAC movement first gave rise to WID or WTL. Fortunately, there's no need for us to distinguish carefully among these ideas. My goal here is to convey a general understanding of the principles underlying writing across the curriculum. So, as we consider a brief history of the WAC movement's development, it will suffice to paint in the details with broad strokes.

A BRIEF HISTORY OF WRITING ACROSS THE CURRICULUM

Today many colleges and universities have strong WAC and WID programs. These programs often feature a generous number of "writing-intensive" courses, which offer students chances to write in a wide variety of settings. These programs are often highly valued by university administrators, and instructors may be given regular opportunities to take part in training programs to help them teach writing in their courses. WAC is everywhere on the academic map.

This wasn't always the case. For years writing played a subsidiary part in disciplinary coursework. Before the late nineteenth century, most American colleges fulfilled a role similar to that of modern liberal arts institutions, with highly generalized course offerings that granted students holistic interdisciplinary training. Disciplinary specialization at the undergraduate level was rare.

Much of this changed in the second half of the nineteenth century. Many of the institutions founded during the post–Civil War period were modeled on the German university, in which disciplinary courses were collected in distinct departments. At such schools, after taking an initial year or two of courses in a school's "core curriculum," students would specialize by enrolling in courses designed to give them expertise in a particular field.

Then, as is the case today, each discipline had its own form of rhetoric and writing. Neither in the disciplines nor in the general curriculum were students given specific instruction in writing, rhetoric, or composition. Rather, it was simply assumed that students would enter college knowing how to write well and that their disciplinary writing skills would develop through imitation and practice.

This system functioned well as long as most students came to college with a secondary education that equipped them with solid communication skills. The system began to falter when college education became accessible to a broader segment of the population, many of whom lacked the pre-college preparation the social elite had had. The generations of college students entering school in the late nineteenth and early twentieth centuries were often less well prepared to write at the level their instructors expected. These students needed help to bring their writing skills up to college level.

In the 1920s and '30s, teachers of writing began to recognize the difficulty of inculcating solid writing skills in the few short months of a first-year composition course. To become effective writers, students would need many opportunities to write, and in many different settings. In the widely read *English Journal*, Oscar J. Campbell of Columbia University wrote an article, "The Failure of Freshman English," attacking the mechanistic methods of writing instruction applied in first-year composition courses and calling for a more diversified and distributed writing curriculum (1939).

It was in this culture that communications studies, and more specifically composition studies, now often called "composition and rhetoric," was born.

Scholars found connections between language and critical thought and began to recognize that language is more than a means of communicating; it is also a means of thinking, learning, and understanding. This point was made by thinkers like Lev Vygotsky (1962) and Piaget (2002). For instance, Vygotsky distinguished between egocentric speech and socialized speech in children. While the latter is meant to communicate with others, according to Vygotsky the function of the former is "thinking aloud, keeping a running accompaniment, as it were to whatever [the child] may be doing" (1962, p. 15). He goes on to assert that egocentric speech does not remain an accompaniment; rather it soon becomes an "instrument of thought" as the speaker begins to plot out solutions to whatever problem is presented him (p. 16). In this way language plays an integral part in critical thought, problem solving, and concept formation. Vygotsky placed special emphasis on the development of scientific concepts, the subject of an entire chapter of *Thought and Language.*

Much of the work on the cognitive potential of writing was going on outside of the United States. James Britton (1970) and his contemporaries in British composition studies introduced their ideas to an American audience in the late 1960s. These scholars placed great value on what Britton called "expressive writing," writing through which the author could articulate and organize his own personal experience, in contrast with the more traditional "transactional" writing. This latter kind of writing is concerned with persuasion. It requires a strong thesis that is defended with argumentation and evidence. Expressive writing champions exploration, thought, and discovery. It is informal, unstructured, and even playful. It is writing done to learn.

Throughout the 1970s and '80s attention was paid to the cognitive benefits of specific writing tasks (note taking, for instance). Experts on academic writing soon recognized that students who engaged in "active" study practices, like outlining, summary writing, or guided journaling, learned course content more fully than students who merely read or studied without taking notes. Soon composition scholars like Britton, Janet Emig, Toby Fulwiler, and Peter Elbow led others in the development of countless low-stakes writing techniques.

During those same decades, administrative support for WAC programs increased substantially. With Carleton College's foundation of a formal WAC program in 1975, the WAC movement began to receive "official" recognition by leaders in postsecondary institutions. In the next few years several other colleges and universities started similar programs (Maimon, 1982). While it enjoyed newfound success, the movement also suffered from growing pains, as it was hard for proponents of WAC to stay in touch with one another. A grassroots movement had become global, but the many disconnected communities within it had yet to find an efficient means of keeping in contact. Moreover, as Elaine Maimon (1982) pointed out, even ardent WAC adherents had to overcome their tendencies to work in isolation from one another. Nonetheless, she closed her essay on a hopeful note: "We have developed strong momentum for our explorations. These explorations beyond our own disciplinary boundaries have helped us to understand our home territory more richly" (p. 72).

That momentum remains, and with it the WAC movement has made great strides in recent years. Since the mid-1970s, hundreds of schools have instituted WAC programs, and the faculty and staff in these programs enjoy the benefits of a stronger-than-ever communication network. Several academic journals (such as *WAC Journal* and *Across the Disciplines*) publish a wide variety of scholarship related to WAC. Regular conferences on WAC (such as the biannual International Writing Across the Curriculum Conference) offer scholars from all disciplines a chance to share their ideas with one another. Websites like the WAC Clearinghouse (maintained by Colorado State University at wac.colostate.edu) collect WAC resources and make them available to teachers and researchers around the world.

WRITING IN THE DISCIPLINES AND WRITING-TO-LEARN IN QUANTITATIVE FIELDS

Where do the quantitative disciplines fit into this picture? Writing across the curriculum may put those of us who work in quantitative fields in an unfamiliar place, but that place is one from which we can achieve tremendous potential. Incorporating writing into our courses gives us room to expand our roles as instructors of our disciplines. It makes us better teachers and our students better learners. Much of the rest of the book is devoted to describing more fully the ways writing can fit neatly and naturally into our classrooms.

Getting involved in WAC gives us a way to enter into productive conversations with our colleagues in other disciplines across our campuses. Writing's centrality in more "qualitative" disciplines has long been acknowledged, and conversations about writing have been going on among these disciplines' practitioners for a long time. However, there are empty seats at the table when these conversations take place. Although traditionally writing-intensive fields are well represented, often missing are the voices of those of us in the quantitative disciplines.

Absent from those conversations, we fail to learn about new ways writing can be used as a tool for teaching and learning. And our colleagues in other disciplines get an incomplete picture of writing in our fields. When we're not in on the conversation, we can't make a case for our kind of writing. How can we expect outsiders to know what writing looks like to us, or if we use writing at all, if we don't take the time to tell them?

What WAC *Is* in Quantitative Fields, and What It *Is Not*

We cannot create authentic writing assignments in the quantitative disciplines simply by using the assignments faculty use in other fields. We can't simply swipe an assignment from a traditionally writing-intensive course in history or literature and expect it to work in a calculus course or a chemistry lab. Although some labels used elsewhere ("research paper," for instance) might apply to the writing we expect our students to do, the writing to which those labels are applied is very different. Why should we expect a research paper in women's studies or cultural anthropology to look anything like a research paper in solid-state physics or mathematical finance?

Rather, we must do a bit more work. We need to help ourselves and our students to re-envision writing so that we understand the role of writing in our own fields. We need to understand the forms that writing can take, and this means understanding the purposes for which we write. Do we write to explain, to communicate, or to clarify? Certain forms of writing lend themselves nicely to these purposes. Or, do we write to learn or to explore? Other, very different, forms of writing will play a part here. No one else is better qualified than we are to do this reimagining of writing, for no one else knows better than us how our kind of writing is done.

This may sound like a lot of work, but it isn't. We don't have to reinvent writing from scratch. Rather, we can draw upon a large body of literature on writing processes and on responding to and assessing writing. We can adapt any of a great number of assignments and exercises that have been developed by others. These adaptations are not effortless ones, and you'll likely need some practice to do them well, but they do save a lot of time and effort.

Writing in the Quantitative Disciplines

When we introduce our students to authentic disciplinary writing, we introduce them to the disciplines themselves. In doing the kind of writing that we do in our own work, students become real practitioners of our disciplines. Authentic writing assignments bring students into a community of scholars by helping the students learn to speak that community's language. It's difficult to imagine how students could be brought into a learning community without first learning how that community's members write.

Let me give you an example. Many of my first-year math majors come to college hoping to study math because they enjoyed taking derivatives in their high school calculus courses or because they're intrigued by the carefulness of geometric proofs. As far as these students know, math is all about computation and calculation, and it has very little to do with communicating ideas. Almost without exception these students struggle when they reach their first "proofs" course. Here, for the first time, they're expected to construct clearly worded justifications for all of the operations they've taken for granted in the past. These justifications must be meaningful not only to the students themselves but to others as well, and the only way they can convey meaning is by learning to write as a mathematician would.

I am sure students in your own discipline experience similar transitions. Up to a certain point in their careers students have been outsiders, or at best infrequent visitors. Much of the work they have done in your discipline has had little context. They've done whatever computing they've done for the sake of computing and not to solve real problems. That is, they have not entered into the larger conversations about your discipline that are taking place beyond their classroom and beyond their campus. Up to this point they have been dabbing their toes into the water at the shore of a deep disciplinary ocean, and now they are being asked to dive in. From this point on, as they grow more practiced at writing like professionals in your field write, they become authentic members of a recognized learning community. More strongly still, they truly become practitioners of your discipline. If you suspect that I'm exaggerating, look at it from a purely pragmatic point of view: if a person writes, for example, like a statistician, speaks like a statistician, and thinks like a statistician, how can you call that person anything but a statistician, if only a relatively inexperienced one?

Of course, even the most earnest students will likely take many years to grow practiced enough at writing and speaking to engage smoothly with their new community of scholars. However, providing students with authentic writing assignments helps them to begin to think like members of this community. These are exactly the sort of assignments WID demands that we give to our students. In a proof-writing course, students must expect to write proofs. In quantitative courses, students must expect to write lab reports, technical reports, research papers, and more—whatever kinds of writing are appropriate to the disciplines those courses deal with.

In the phrase "authentic writing assignments" I include genres with very specific purposes and audiences, like those I've just mentioned, but I also include other kinds of disciplinary writing as well. We cannot focus on such narrowly defined writing-in-the-disciplines tasks. (There is no shortage of style guides and "how-to" books that give deep and detailed direction on writing in discipline-specific genres. I've included lists of recommendations at the end of this chapter and at the end of the book. Any attempt to condense or summarize these books would do them a disservice.) Instead, we must focus on any activities that help the writer get a handle on typical disciplinary writing tasks, including not only the traditional genres but also any and all of the low-stakes writing activities involved in writing-to-learn.

WTL in the Quantitative Disciplines

WTL activities are as critical in quantitative disciplines as they are in more traditionally writing-intensive fields. After all, many of the low-stakes exploratory writing activities that can help a student of history reflect on the consequences of war in the Persian Gulf can just as easily help a student of physical chemistry puzzle out the physical interactions between electron orbitals. The formal writing a student does in producing a term paper or original research article on these orbitals communicates ideas to others, but it is the hundreds of pages of scratchwork, research log entries, notes-to-self, and other "coffee shop napkin" pieces of writing that helped the author to generate and make sense of those ideas in the first place.

Let me give you another example, one that demonstrates how informal writing can be used to help assess student learning even as it promotes that learning. For several years when I first began teaching, I used formal writing exercises to probe calculus students' understanding of important ideas like the Mean Value Theorem or the definition of a continuous function. For instance, I would ask students short-answer questions about these ideas on quizzes and exams, and I would require that they write brief essay-style summaries of the ideas as homework. These assessment efforts were largely unsuccessful, for even the strongest responses to these exercises offered a narrow view of the students' understanding. In their short-answer responses the students would often parrot the technical definitions they'd memorized from the textbook. In their essays the students might expand on these definitions a little more fully, but their language was still clinical, detached, and voiceless. Although it's important that my students learn to use technical terms carefully and correctly, these exercises were meant to help me get at the students' intuitive grasp on course concepts, not to test their memory of textbook definitions.

A few years ago I tried a new approach: I began asking students to write dialogues. Here each student writes a transcript of a conversation between herself and her "best friend, also enrolled in our course," in which the student assumes the role of the expert, helping her confused friend puzzle through whatever course concept the dialogue treats. Of course, the student writes the lines for her imaginary friend as well, and through this character's words she can safely express her own misgivings and confusion about the ideas she's writing about. I ask the student to avoid technical terms and notation whenever possible, using instead the everyday conversational language she would use to explain a new idea to a friend who may not yet be as knowledgeable as she is. This helps the student develop her intuitive understanding even as she's communicating that understanding to me through the dialogue.

The dialogue exercises have been helpful and well received. Students often find them corny at first, but they also find them challenging. After all, few of them have been asked to explain math in everyday words before. The exercises are excellent opportunities to explore ideas with little or no consequence to the students' grades, and by the semester's end most students come to recognize the dialogues' value as tools for learning.

Maybe you too find the idea of writing a dialogue about continuous functions, or covariance, or quantum mechanics a little corny. However, the dialogue exercise is only one of dozens of low-stakes writing activities you might use:

- To help students explore new concepts without stumbling over ideas they don't fully understand, ask them to *freewrite*, writing without stopping and without editing their work, for several minutes. For example, "Write nonstop for five minutes on the sampling methods one might use to survey students' views on science education."

- To help students begin to blend quantitative information (formulas, graphs, and numerical data sets) and qualitative information, ask them to draw a "poster" illustrating the relationships between the quantitative elements of their work and the qualitative description of those elements they'd give to someone else. For example, "Draw a poster explaining the interaction between supply curves and demand curves."

- To help students develop the intuition needed to compute with unwieldy or unfamiliar quantities, ask them to write "estimation essays" in which they must apply methods from your course to come up with approximate solutions to poorly posed problems. For example, "Explain how to use Riemann sums to obtain a rough estimate of the number of gumballs contained in a candy machine."

- To help students summarize succinctly the central ideas of complicated concepts, ask them to write in a familiar form that is strongly constrained in length. For example, "Write a Twitter tweet (140 characters, at most) describing Newton's Laws of Motion."

As these examples show, writing-to-learn is just as powerful a learning tool in quantitative disciplines as it is in any other.

CHALLENGES TO IMPLEMENTING WAC IN QUANTITATIVE FIELDS

I do need to be clear about one thing: incorporating writing activities and assignments into your courses will not be an effortless task. If you're to make the most of the opportunities writing offers you may need to make changes in the way you teach, and some of these changes challenge long-standing assumptions you may have about teaching and learning.

Moreover, there are challenges specific to the quantitative disciplines. For instance, the rarified technical language of many quantitative disciplines lends itself poorly to paraphrasing, making it difficult for beginning writers to get a grip on unfamiliar terms and notation even in informal low-stakes writing. For example, the technical definition of a continuous function often given in a first-semester calculus course might read as follows:

A function f is said to be *continuous* at a point a in its domain if for any number $\varepsilon > 0$ there is a number $\delta > 0$ such that for any x in f's domain, $0 < |x - a| < \delta$ implies $|f(x) - f(a)| < \varepsilon$.

I count at least three technical terms here (not including the word *number*, which could easily be included in this list), three distinct mathematical operations or relations expressed symbolically, and two potentially unfamiliar letters. Even the brightest math majors may take two or three years to fully grasp the subtleties of this definition, and at first few students can do much more than repeat the definition word for word when asked to summarize it. Mathematics has no monopoly on such dense terminology and notation; they're found in any quantitative discipline in rich supply. One of the toughest challenges in helping students learn to write in these disciplines is to help make sense of such terms.

There is a related difficulty. To a greater extent than in many other fields, writing in the quantitative disciplines relies heavily on visual elements (graphs and charts) and numerical elements (functions, formulas, and tables of data) that are hard to weave into traditional written narratives. Incorporating these elements into authentic disciplinary writing is difficult. Incorporating them into writing-to-learn activities can be just as hard.

Perhaps the most daunting obstacle impeding writing instruction in quantitative fields is resistance, even hostility, to writing. Our students, many of whom go into quantitative fields because they expect to do little writing there, may have a hard time understanding how central writing is to the work in these fields. More critically, though, we may have to fight against faculty resistance, some of it our own. Although it's hard to deny that we all do a good deal of writing, it's easier to assume that training our students to write is not our business, especially when we've got so much content already crammed into our courses. If we're going to make writing work in the ways I describe in the later chapters, we need to face this resistance and deal with it.

Overcoming Faculty Resistance

During the past few decades the center of attention in the college classroom has shifted from the teacher to the student. The instructor of the past was described as a "sage on the stage." In this role the instructor showed off his disciplinary expertise, demonstrating knowledge to his students, who dutifully took notes or responded to the instructor's questions when asked to do so. The set-up of the classroom was clear: the instructor was there to teach, and the students were there to learn. In this scenario, the students, far less knowledgeable and experienced than their instructor, had little to offer to the conversation, so they spoke infrequently.

Today the instructor is more frequently described as a "guide on the side." The instructor still plays an important part, but it's a more supportive or facilitative role. The students now take center stage, and they are expected to become more active participants in the generation of knowledge. The students are no longer outsiders with nothing to contribute to the class's conversation. They are now themselves meaning-makers and active practitioners of their disciplines. The instructor stands at the students' sides as they begin to explore new ideas, and his experience in his field helps him facilitate his students' exploration.

WAC principles are much more at home in the latter sort of classroom. Indeed, authentic writing assignments make more sense when students are already being asked to think like practitioners of their disciplines, and writing-to-learn exercises give students the tools they need to engage in guided exploration. Many faculty members are comfortable with this new pedagogical paradigm and will need little convincing to put WAC to work in their courses. (I've found younger faculty members the most receptive to WAC ideas. This isn't surprising, for it stands to reason that those faculty who themselves learned in student-centered classrooms are generally more comfortable with WAC.) However, some faculty resist WAC ideas strongly, especially in the quantitative disciplines, where writing has never been as central as computational content.

How can this resistance best be met? Here are a few suggestions that may help.

- *Recognize that WAC principles are effective ones.* WAC will help students feel at home in their disciplines and more easily master that discipline's ideas. Writing in the disciplines does more than help students feel like members of a specific learning community; it helps them become members of that community. Meanwhile writing-to-learn gives students new tools to tinker with as they prod and probe the ideas put before them. Writing will help them learn better, and if taught to write in their disciplines, they will more clearly communicate the ideas they learn.

- *Recognize that WAC principles need not be difficult to adopt.* Though you may need to make some adjustments to your courses, these adjustments are not insurmountable ones. Keep in mind that sometimes very little change is needed, especially if your goal is not to create a writing-intensive course but only to introduce a few simple writing activities; this can be done in little more than a few minutes a day. Even when more substantial change is called for, that change can take place incrementally, over time. Moreover, there are already models for many of the changes you may end up making, and you'll rarely have to start from scratch.

- *Recognize how fun and fulfilling WAC can be.* Most quantitative disciplines are problem based, and many of us get into these fields because we enjoy the challenge of a puzzling problem. Viewed in a certain way, implementing WAC activities can seem like problems to be solved. Many writing-to-learn activities, in particular, are playful and game-like. I've rarely had more fun in my teaching than when guiding students in activities like writing letters from the point of view of Renaissance mathematicians such as Newton and Gauss or condensing convoluted definitions down to 140 characters or less. Moreover, nothing is more fulfilling than comparing the writing students do at the end of a term with the writing they did at the term's beginning; sometimes the progress the students make in discovering, analyzing, and expressing their ideas through writing is nothing short of amazing.

If you're new to teaching writing, it's understandable if you're uncomfortable about incorporating it into your courses. After all, writing takes time, practice, and patience both for you and for your students. However, you need not spend too much time when you first introduce writing. Keep in mind that you don't need to introduce it all at once: you can begin with a few simple exercises here and there, and in many cases you need do no more than this. Unless you plan on making your course a writing-intensive one, these exercises may suffice. I am confident that no matter what sort of writing you introduce your students to, you will see improvement in your students' communication skills and conceptual understanding.

Faculty are not the only ones who may resist. Students in quantitative fields are reluctant to write and often insist that they do it poorly: "That's why I got into this subject. . . . I don't write well!" Here students run the risk of self-fulfilling prophecy, for the more they resist writing, the less practiced they will be, and as with anything else, practice at writing is needed for improvement. I close this chapter with an attempt to understand and overcome students' resistance to writing.

"Why Are My Students So Focused on Finding the Answer?"

Writing isn't something that's made; it's something that's done. It's an action, and not an object. It's a process, and not merely a product. Yet often this isn't how students think of writing, especially students in the quantitative disciplines. These fields are problem centered, and students spend much of their time seeking solutions to problems posed to them. Although students may understand that they must write to communicate their solutions to these problems, their focus is not on writing clearly but on making sure that they've found the right solution to the problem. Their writing often suffers because it's done as an afterthought, literally, after the solution is known. To many students in our disciplines, writing is the end result of uninspired hours of recording facts. Why do they see it in this way? If we can learn to recognize the reasons our students resist disciplinary writing, we can learn how better to overcome their resistance.

Obscuring Process   Sadly, we are often the ones who lead our students to privilege the product over the process. We insist on quantitative correctness and logical rigor. We congratulate the students who are most skilled at finding the solutions to the problems we pose, regardless of how those solutions are obtained. Our priorities are evidenced by the prevalence of standardized multiple choice exams at every level of science education, from elementary school through the Graduate Record Exams. These exams obscure process altogether, placing all value on the unambiguous and objective end result.

Moreover, most models of disciplinary writing to which we expose our students regularly downplay the process through which they were crafted. Take a look at the textbooks we use. Though we can hardly expect texts in mathematics, statistics, or physical chemistry to present unpolished exposition, we may at least wish that these books offered a window on the discovery process that led to the facts and formulas filling the books' pages. However, even this process is largely invisible in most textbooks, and the places in which the process appears are exceptional enough to prove the rule. A thorough discussion on the manner in which the history of science is obscured by the very people who advance that history can be found in Thomas Kuhn's *The Structure of Scientific Revolutions* (1962), but it's not hard to find everyday examples of this obscuring.

Consider, for example, a typical calculus textbook written for an undergraduate audience. The bulk of most such books consist of definitions, theorems, and proofs, interspersed with examples, graphs, and figures demonstrating the definitions and applications of the theorems. The authors of these books take pains to begin with simple concepts and work up to more complicated ones, indicating when necessary the ways each new concept follows logically on the last. Though a clever student might see traces of a discovery process in this record of facts, the process is rarely foregrounded explicitly. Occasionally these texts mention the name of a great scholar and may include a small picture or the dates marking the scholar's life span, but more regularly they put this material at the end of a section or chapter or they literally marginalize it by placing it off on the side of the page. Even more rare are those texts that mention an insight that led the scholar to the discovery detailed in the book's main text.

As another example, consider academic articles, another sort of writing we often place before our students. These are no better and may be even worse models of the writing process. These articles represent the cutting edge of our scholarly knife, so we might expect them to give a robust record of the discovery process in action. However, as Scott L. Montgomery (1996) points out, in such articles the scientist tends to cast her discoveries as inevitable and timeless, with no hint of the human in those discoveries. Such articles drone on in "the purged voice of a coherent, harmonious, and successful investigation. . . . What seems to appear is Truth, not a claim for it; the Scientist, not a particular individual; Data, not writing" (p. 13). The scientist hides the discovery process, obliterating the personal struggles, stumbling blocks, and obstacles over which she tripped as she worked away in her lab or at her desk, effectively portraying discovery as though it were a smooth and unobstructed road.

Obscuring Agency   Moreover, the scientist does all that she can to eliminate herself as an agent of discovery. Montgomery points out that the emergence of the personal in scientific writing is typically viewed as a failure on the part of the author, who must always be concerned with maintaining "heroic objectivity" (p. 18). This is strongly evident in quantitative fields, where the passive voice predominates and the author uses more and more precise technical terminology, making the language as denotative and unambiguous as possible.

It hasn't always been like this. Until relatively recently much scientific writing bore unmistakable traces of the human being who crafted it: personal observations, unproven speculations, and excerpts from great works of literature peppered scientific prose (see Montgomery, 1996, pp. 26–31). In these traces we can glimpse the process that underlies discovery. After all, untested speculations may be places where the author has become stuck at some point in the process, while personal anecdotes and literary references may mark the author's attempt to get unstuck by reflecting on experiences common to us all.

The act of writing-to-discover is not a surprising one. As our discussion of writing-to-learn shows, writing is more than a means of recording ideas: writing helps the writer think through ideas. Writing is a tool for learning, and a tool for discovering. Thus when we encourage our students to engage in a writing process, we invite them into a community of discoverers. They are no longer simply passive recipients of knowledge we try to pass on to them: they are now active creators of that knowledge.

Overcoming Student Resistance

I spend most of Chapter Two demonstrating how writing can be thought of as a process, each step of which helps the writer craft a better final product. Encouraging our students to engage in this writing process will help them become creators. Moreover, the quality of the written work our students produce will improve tremendously once they've begun to recognize and apply this writing process. They will take care to make their writing clearer, more complete, and more well composed.

How can we begin to overcome our students' resistance to this writing process? Here are some general guidelines.

- *Help students give structure to writing.* We can make engaging in the process easier by structuring writing assignments in ways that make the steps of the process clear. Just as we teach our students how to solve difficult problems in math, physics, and chemistry by breaking them down into more manageable "subproblems," we can teach students how to become better writers by breaking writing assignments into manageable stages. Once our students realize that no single stage in the process is tremendously difficult, they will be more apt to use the process more regularly.

- *Give students models of authentic writing.* We can also offer our students more models for disciplinary writing than the standard genres of textbooks and academic articles. If we ask them to read, and better yet to write, documents that do not belong to one of these genres, we can help them to see more clearly the ways discovery is done in our disciplines. As we will see, there is virtually no limit to the variety of forms of writing we can ask our students to create.

- *Don't get hung up on correctness.* We do well to deemphasize correctness, at least enough so that students don't lose sight of the importance of clarity in communication. I do not mean to say that finding the right answer isn't important, only that it's often no more important than being able to convey that answer to someone else effectively. After all, having the right answer is meaningless if you're not able to make it clear to your colleagues.

I hope that this chapter has helped to answer some basic questions about writing in the quantitative disciplines. In particular, before moving onto more concrete questions like "How to write?" and "What to write?" I've tried to address the question "Why write in the first place?" Put simply, we write to communicate and we write to learn. This is no less the case in quantitative disciplines than it is in other, more traditionally writing-intensive, fields. If students are to become practitioners of a particular field, they must be given the chance to write authentically in that field, and they must learn to think like scholars in that field. Writing across the curriculum, through writing in the disciplines and writing-to-learn, meets both of these goals. Our next step is to lay out a practical plan for helping writing to happen.

READINGS AND RESOURCES

You can find a much fuller account of the WAC movement's history in *Reference Guide to Writing Across the Curriculum* (2005) by Charles Bazerman et al.; "Writing Across the Curriculum: Past, Present, and Future" (1982) by Elaine Maimon (appearing in *Teaching Writing in All Disciplines*, C. Williams Griffin, ed.); and *Writing in the Academic Disciplines, 1870–1990: A Curricular History* (1991) by David R. Russell. John C. Brereton's collection of primary sources, *The Origin of Composition Studies in the American College, 1875–1925: A Documentary History* (1995), provides a fascinating look at the early years of formal composition instruction at the college level.

Meanwhile, Lev Vygotsky's seminal work *Thought and Language* (1962) outlines the connections between writing and thinking that served as the basis for the writing-to-learn movement that developed later in the twentieth century. James Britton's *Language and Learning* (1970) makes the implications of these connections more explicit still. These books lay out the theory behind the practice of academic writing.

For more information on discipline-specific genres (the products of traditional writing in the disciplines), the following sources offer a great deal of direction. Additional recommendations appear in the Recommended Reading and Resources section at the end of the book.

Computer Science

Perelman, L. C., Paradis, J., and Barrett, E. *The Mayfield Handbook of Technical and Scientific Writing*. Palo Alto, CA: Mayfield Publishing, 1998.

Zobel, J. *Writing for Computer Science* (2nd ed.). New York: Springer-Verlag, 2004.

Economics

McCloskey, D. N. *Economical writing* (2nd ed.). Prospect Heights, IL: Waveland Press, 2000.

Engineering

Silyn-Roberts, H. *Writing for Science and Engineering: Papers, Presentations, and Reports.* Oxford, UK: Butterworth-Heinemann, 2000.

Sorby, S. A., and Bulleit, W. M. *An Engineer's Guide to Technical Communication.* Upper Saddle River, NJ: Pearson Prentice Hall, 2006.

Mathematics

Gerver, R. K. *Writing Math Research Papers: A Guide for Students and Instructors.* Emeryville, CA: Key Curriculum Press, 2007.

Gillman, L. *Writing Mathematics Well: A Manual for Authors.* Washington, DC: Mathematical Association of America, 1987.

Krantz, S. G. *A Primer of Mathematical Writing: Being a Disquisition on Having Your Ideas Recorded.* Providence, RI: American Mathematical Society, 1997.

General Quantitative Sciences

Alley, M. *The Craft of Scientific Writing* (3rd ed.). New York: Springer Science+Business Media, 1996.

Higham, N. J. *Handbook of Writing for the Mathematical Sciences.* Philadelphia: Society for Industrial and Applied Mathematics, 1993.

O'Connor, M. *Writing Successfully in Science.* London and New York: E & FN Spon, 1991.

Peat, J., Elliott, E., Baur, L., and Keena, V. *Scientific Writing: Easy When You Know How.* London: BMJ Books, 2002.

Pera, M., and Shea, W. (eds). *Persuading Science: The Art of Scientific Rhetoric.* Canton, MA: Science History Publishers, 1991.

Writing as a Process

For many reasons, all of us write in our professional lives. We craft assignments, articles, agendas for committees, grants, referee reports, book reviews, monographs, manuscripts, mission statements, lectures, lesson plans, textbooks, and official emails of almost endless variety. Before we deem them fit for sharing publicly, we draft, review, and redraft nearly every one of these pieces once, twice, or many more times. I write this very sentence knowing that before this book goes to press these words will be read by no fewer than a dozen pairs of careful eyes. Moreover, I know there is a possibility these words will not appear in the final version of the book at all.

Every one of us who writes for any public purpose expects to do a considerable amount of preparation and organization before careful writing begins. The seeking out, sorting, and synthesis of ideas is a key part of the writing process for us, and we often use writing to help us think those ideas through. Moreover, we know that as we write we will likely have to pause and reorganize our thoughts before we continue, often many times over. Every time we change our minds, we change our writing. We know that review and revision are indispensible steps we must take when crafting a piece of writing meant to be shared with more than a few others. In doing all of this we recognize what our students often do not, at least at first: that writing is a process and not a product. Put another way, writing is something we do and not simply something we make.

I begin this chapter with a brief examination of one of the more stereotypical genres of writing in the quantitative disciplines: the mathematical proof. My purpose here is to show that even so abstract a form of writing as a proof corresponds to a cohesive writing process we can indicate to our students as we help them learn to write.

I then lay out some of the steps of that process more carefully. These steps are both broad and general and take different forms for different writers and for different writing projects. It is rare that a writer will follow the process in lock-step every time he writes. The writing process is often nonlinear, and the writer may find himself revisiting some of these steps over and over. The looseness of the process has led some scholars to claim that there really is no such thing as a "writing process" after all! (See Kent, 1999, for a collection of several such views.) Nevertheless, your students will likely benefit from a basic understanding of the steps we consider here, as this will assist them in discovering and developing their ideas as they write.

Finally, I point out ways we can structure writing in our courses to help our students get the most out of the writing process. We can design our individual writing assignments so that they mirror the stages of the process, helping students to recognize those stages. We can arrange for multiple writing assignments in a single course to build upon one another to help students meet increasingly challenging writing goals as the students' familiarity with the writing process grows. Sometimes we can even sequence writing assignments from course to course, recognizing how the sophistication of students' writing grows over a longer period of time. Such sequencing helps us as much as it helps our students, for the structure it provides makes our departments and programs stronger and better able to fulfill their academic missions.

THE PROCESS AT WORK IN A MATHEMATICAL PROOF

I begin unpacking the writing process by examining how it underlies even one of the most rarified sorts of scientific prose: the mathematical proof. On its face, a *proof* is a step-by-step logical or computational justification of a mathematical assertion, often drawing on prior proofs for its logical force. (For example, consider the proof in the textbox justifying the claim "The sum of two even integers is again an even integer.") Proofs, like lab reports in chemistry or biology, and like technical reports in statistics or engineering, are examples of "apprenticeship genres" (Carter, Ferzli, & Wiebe, 2007), genres learned through direct engagement with disciplinary ideas. Let's take a moment to deconstruct the proof genre and see whether we can identify the steps of the process the "prover" uses to help him write a proof.

The sum of two even integers is again an even integer.

Recall that we say an integer n is *even* if there is an integer s such that $n = 2s$. Suppose that m and n are even. Thus there are integers s and t such that $m = 2s$ and $n = 2t$. Therefore $m + n = 2s + 2t = 2(s + t)$, using the fact that multiplication distributes over addition. Letting k be the integer $s + t$, we see that $m + n = 2k$, so that it is indeed even, as desired. Since m and n were arbitrary even integers, we are done.

Imre Lakatos reminds us that we fall victim to mathematical formalism if we assume that a proof is nothing more than the logical justification of a mathematical claim. In *Proofs and Refutations* (1976), Lakatos sets up a conversation among a teacher and several of his students. Initially this conversation focuses on the proof of a particular geometric claim. Very quickly, though, the conversation moves to address the very nature of proof itself. Lakatos's "Teacher" character lectures his class on the foolishness of defining proof too narrowly: "You are interested only in proofs which 'prove' what they have set out to prove. I am interested in proofs even if they do not accomplish their intended task. Columbus did not reach India but he discovered something quite interesting" (p. 14).

Here Lakatos recognizes that for a skilled mathematician, a proof is more than a piece of finished writing, and more than a listing of the logical steps the prover takes in verifying a statement's truth. There's much more to a polished proof than what we see on the page. If we could see them, earlier drafts of the proof would show us errors, gaps, and indecision as the prover tried to write his way past whatever mathematical obstacles he encountered. Now and then, finding an obstacle insurmountable, the prover may have had to abandon a draft altogether, starting anew with a fresh attempt. At the unseen early stages of writing a proof, the prover is writing to generate ideas and writing to make sense of those ideas. Put in terms we've used already, he is doing writing-to-learn.

For simple proofs, this first stage may take only minutes; for difficult ones it may take years. At some point, however, the prover takes whatever cluttered and chaotic notes he has and tries to make sense of them by arranging his data into lists or by creating outlines of his ideas. With these lists and outlines to guide him, the prover then tries to flesh his ideas out and match them up with one another, writing as he goes. Although he may not write his proof from start to finish, gradually his disparate ideas grow together. As they do so, the prover rearranges his writing, moving the corresponding passages into their proper places relative to one another and smoothing out the transitions that tie them together.

Once he's produced a rough draft of a proof, the prover may ask a colleague to take a look at his work, to see whether it makes sense. Is it correct? Is it complete? Does it adhere to the stylistic conventions of discipline? Perhaps most important, will it be clear to the audience that will eventually read it? His colleague's feedback will help the prover redraft his work, maybe more than once. In fact, several iterations may be necessary before the prover feels comfortable making his work public.

From start to finish, the prover took several steps.

1. *Prewriting to generate ideas.* This first step has all of the elements of writing-to-learn: it is informal and often unshared. The goal here is to come up with ideas, not to explain them clearly to others.

2. *Organizing and outlining.* In the next step the prover puts his initial thoughts into some sort of order. More informal writing takes place here.

3. *Drafting, reviewing, and revising.* "Real" writing can begin once the prover has given his initial thoughts some structure. This writing can be revised according to feedback from others.

Once a completed draft is done and all major changes have been made, the prover will likely go back over what he's written and correct minor mistakes in punctuation or notation. As we should make clear to our students, the very last round of editing need not and should not take place until all major revisions are completed. After all, fixing the punctuation in a paragraph that gets removed in revision is about as worthwhile as polishing the candlesticks on the *Titanic*.

THE WRITING PROCESS

There is nothing special about the genre of the mathematical proof. In fact, as was pointed out forty years ago (see Emig, 1971, and Murray, 1972), a process much like the one outlined will apply to many kinds of writing we do, from the simplest to the most complex. Of course, we do well to remember that the steps of this process may take different forms for different kinds of writing, and for different disciplines. Prewriting, drafting, and revision all look different in a first-year chemistry course than they do in a senior-level economics seminar.

We also do well to keep in mind that there are as many different kinds of writers as there are different kinds of writing. For many people, writing is a highly nonlinear activity in which they revisit, often many times over, the various stages in the process I describe here. You should help your students to understand that while adhering to the process can give them structure and help to guide their writing, they may not mechanistically follow every step of the process every time they are asked to write. Once they've completed several writing projects, you might even consider asking your students to reflect on their own writing process to see how it compares with the one we encounter following. All steps of the writing process we discuss here are grounded in decades of solid research on composition and are detailed more carefully elsewhere; see for example, Clark (2003); Elbow (1998); Emig (1971); and Timbur (2010).

Prewriting: Seeking Out and Sifting Through Ideas

Some students fail to craft convincing prose because they overlook this critical stage of the writing process. Before any finely polished paragraphs hit the page, a good deal of brainstorming goes on, as well as substantial arrangement and rearrangement of ideas. Moreover, it is in this stage of the process that the writer should ask questions that help her identify certain key rhetorical elements of the writing she's about to create. For what purpose am I writing, and how will that shape what I have to say? For what audience am I writing, and in what form or genre should I write to reach that audience? What tone should I strike when writing in that genre?

Despite the use of the term *prewriting*, a good deal of writing, often informal in nature, can go on in this initial stage. In fact, many of the informal writing activities we will encounter later can be used to help students begin to get their ideas out on the page before more careful arrangement of ideas begins. I mention a few of these activities here, as they are particularly effective at generating ideas before taking on a complicated writing project. These activities are often playful ones, and at this stage the writer should feel free to play, letting her ideas combine and recombine without restraint. This freedom will encourage new ideas and lead to greater possibilities and potential.

Freewriting Freewriting is a technique originally developed by Peter Elbow in *Writing Without Teachers* (1973). In freewriting, the writer grants herself a fixed amount of time (five minutes, say) during which she will write, nonstop, about a particular topic. Even if she becomes stuck or strays off the topic during the exercise, the writer continues to write about whatever comes to mind, without any regard for spelling, punctuation, or grammar. Visual data (graphs, charts, diagrams) play such an important role in quantitative disciplines that the writer should feel free to include these elements in her freewriting as well.

The goal of this exercise is to eliminate the "in-line" editing that often goes on when we write. This in-line editing censors thoughts that might later turn out to be fruitful ones. While early editing can eliminate dead-end ideas, it can also destroy potential connections, insights, and epiphanies. It is much easier to edit out those dead ends later in the writing process than it is to recover a key insight we lost to premature editing at an earlier stage.

At the start of a more structured writing assignment, the student can use freewriting simply to get her thoughts on out on the page. The student is less likely to dismiss ideas out of hand when freewriting them. Though some of her ideas are likely to be cast aside as she goes back over them and organizes them more carefully, the multiplicity of ideas freewriting helps to generate cannot help but lead to richer writing later in the project.

Clustering Clustering is a prewriting strategy that offers the writer a nonlinear means of organizing his ideas before formal writing begins. The writer starts off with single word or phrase related to the topic of interest, placing it in a bubble at the center of a page. From this point on the writer adds additional words or phrases as they come to him, attaching them to related words or phrases that have already been recorded. A weblike "map" of the topic emerges as more and more ideas are put in place. From the way the ideas are clustered, the writer may begin to see ways his writing can best be organized.

Clustering helps the writer to see connections that were hidden before and can help make sense of very cluttered data. How might clustering be useful in quantitative disciplines? Here are a few examples.

- *For a second-semester calculus course.* "Your team of three must write a textbook section on methods of integration. [See the student-authored textbook project in Chapter Five.] In preparation, use clustering to illustrate the connections between these methods."

- *For a statistics course.* "Collecting the data for your final research project will require you to choose among a number of different sampling methods. Use clustering to illustrate the relationships between various sampling methods."

- *For a materials science course.* "An automaker has commissioned your company to machine the wheel components for its new line of sedans. In constructing the wheels, your company must decide between two alloys with decidedly different properties. Use clustering to create a 'map' of the chemical and physical properties of these two alloys."

How might the result of the first example appear? As a review of prerequisite concepts, students in my second-semester calculus courses often spend the first day of class collaborating to create a map of the first semester of the course. Figure 2.1 shows the map the most recent class came up with.

This exercise is the first step of an assignment asking the students to pair up and write brief explanations of each of the concepts they come up with for their map. The preliminary step we take together in class helps each pair of students situate their write-ups in the larger context of Calculus I. Their writing is clearer and more focused as a result.

Cubing This prewriting strategy, first described by Gregory and Elizabeth Cowan in their book *Writing* (1980), is designed to help writers examine a topic from every several different perspectives before writing about it more fully. The cubing technique is somewhat more rigidly defined than the previous techniques but still offers a great deal of room for play.

In cubing, the six faces of a cube correspond to six means of getting at a topic:

1. *Describe it.* What are its basic attributes?

2. *Compare it.* What is it similar to?

3. *Associate it.* What does it relate to?

4. *Analyze it.* What are its inner workings?

5. *Apply it.* What can it be used for?

6. *Argue for or against it.* Can you make a case for one side or the other, or for both?

These methods of picking apart a given topic were designed with more traditional writing-centered disciplines in mind. Some of these methods are easily applied to quantitative courses. We hope, after all, that our students will be

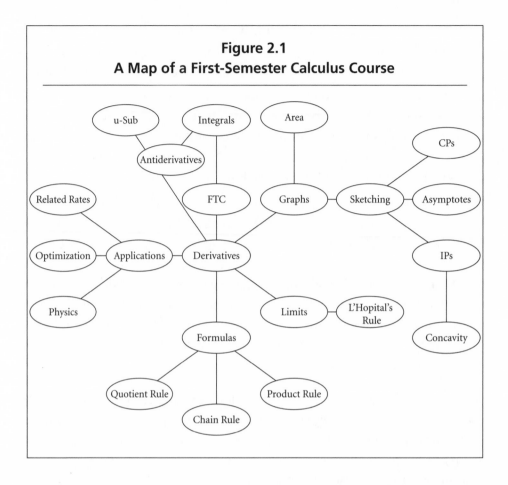

Figure 2.1
A Map of a First-Semester Calculus Course

able both to analyze and to apply the ideas they learn with us. It may be difficult to apply some of the methods to topics students might write about in some of our courses. For instance, how does one argue for or against the Fundamental Theorem of Calculus?

However, meaningful connections are not always arrived at easily, and the stretching students do in applying the cubing methods to their topics may yield remarkable and profound insights. In an argument for the Fundamental Theorem of Calculus, for example, a student might offer substantive justification for using the adjective *fundamental*.

The examples of invention strategies I've mentioned here are just a representative few. If you're interested in learning about more such strategies, Art Peterson's *The Writer's Workout Book: 113 Stretches Toward Better Prose* (1996) offers a wide variety. While Peterson's book focuses on writing instruction at the high school level, many of the invention strategies it addresses are easily adaptable to college classrooms.

All of these prewriting strategies can help students to collect the data relevant to their writing projects before they commence with more structured writing. However, not every strategy does much to organize that data or put it in any meaningful order. This is done in the next step of the writing process.

Organizing and Outlining

The prewriting exercises described here are informal and are designed to help the writer reflect broadly on the subject of his writing as he generates ideas. It can often be a struggle to find ways to make all of these ideas work well with one another, and sometimes the writer must get rid of old ideas or at least adjust them so that they fit with new ones as they come to mind. Which ideas are related to one another? Which are consequences of others? In the end, which ideas are most useful, most relevant, or most true?

Some of the prewriting methods we've looked at help the writer begin to organize his ideas. For instance, clustering illustrates connections between ideas, and cubing groups ideas according to their relationships with the central topic. However, the way these ideas are organized may make it hard to write about them. Most written work (especially that which our students produce) is meant to be read in a linear fashion, while most prewriting strategies offer only non-linear structure. Further organization is often needed before polished writing can begin.

Outlines   One way to accomplish this organization is by creating an outline. Outlines are so familiar to us that they may seem cliché, so we may overlook their usefulness for students who have trouble giving structure to their writing. Yet when students are asked to regiment their ideas into headings, subheadings, and so forth in hierarchical fashion, they become more aware of the connections among those ideas. They find it easier to identify the most important concepts and to understand how subordinate ideas can be organized to support those concepts.

A well-made outline is more than a catalog of the ideas the writer plans to write about. It's a roadmap of the writing project as a whole, and the writer can follow that map as he commences writing. Indeed, the hierarchical structure of a good outline mirrors the structure of the finished piece of writing: the highest-level headings of the outline may correspond to sections in the finished piece, while the subheadings correspond to paragraphs. If the writer has spent some time in working up an easy-to-follow outline, the writing of the paper's first draft may involve little more than fleshing out each of the headings and subheadings more fully and smoothing over the transitions between the resulting paragraphs.

Annotated Bibliographies and Similar Organizational Strategies   While some writing assignments require little research or reading on the student's part, more formal writing projects may require the student to dig a bit more deeply. Even if she has a topic in mind, the student may not yet know enough about that topic to say anything meaningful about it without first doing some searching for sources, evaluating those sources, and understanding the way they relate to one another.

Students who are new to academic writing often have considerable difficulty performing these tasks. They find it hard to evaluate sources' importance, credibility, and relevance. They find it hard to compare the information they gather from different sources and to synthesize this information. They find it hard to use the ideas they've found to formulate and then defend their own ideas. All of this can be said of beginning writers in any academic field. It's all the more true of beginning writers in quantitative disciplines, in which students are generally unaccustomed to writing.

Asking students to write an annotated bibliography can help them with these tasks. An annotated bibliography offers a summary of each source the student has referenced in her work. Since such a document is not common in many quantitative disciplines, you may have some latitude in determining the format of the bibliography you ask your students to produce. Certainly a student should list each source she finds and give a brief summary of the source's main claims. You may ask her to go further, evaluating the credibility of each source (based, for instance, on its age, the medium in which it appeared, or the stature of its author) or comparing it with other sources in her bibliography. You may ask her to reflect on the role each source plays in her own project: Did the source help? How? Did it provide a missing piece of information, or did it give a more thorough description of information found in another source?

Other exercises can help students make sense of the sources they've found in their research. Recognizing the difficulty students have in analyzing their sources, Donna Coghill, Bonnie Orzolek, Faye Prichard, and Laura Westmoreland of

Virginia Commonwealth University (2010) developed new structured organizational strategies to help students through this stage of the writing process. One of their inventive strategies was the "mock conference" assignment designed by Bonnie Orzolek.

This assignment is meant to help students make meaning of the conversation going on among the several authors of the sources the student has found. Orzolek noticed two problems in students' reviews of disciplinary literature: "Students summarize articles sequentially or chronologically instead of comprehensively integrating their findings" and "students extract only glaring differences found in their research, and fail to tease out more subtle differences" (Coghill et al., 2010). She wanted to help them find more meaningful patterns in the information they find in their sources.

Orzolek asks each of her students to imagine herself as the organizer of an academic conference that all of her sources' authors will be attending. One of the student's duties as organizer is to assign seating for the conference banquet. Students must place no more than four attendees at each table, arranging them so that all conference-goers at any given table share interests, information, or concerns. The student must arrange her guests so as to stimulate conversation at each table. Once the seating chart is set, the student must give each of her tables a name that summarizes the common perspective of the authors seated at it. Finally, the student seats herself at one of the tables. This last act challenges her to figure out how her own ideas fit into the bigger picture painted by the scholars who have come before her.

Though especially relevant in disciplines in which scholarly opinions can vary significantly, this exercise can be helpful even in areas in which students' sources are unlikely to offer outright contradictory points of view. For example, a math student writing a research paper will likely find that her sources cluster according to their relevance to her own work and according to the kinds of information they offer her. Some sources may give her the theoretical ideas she'll need to prove her own claims, and others may illustrate the ways these ideas play together. Still others may offer the student concrete applications of the ideas her own paper treats.

Drafting, Reviewing, and Revising

These exercises help students get the most out of their sources, readying them for the next stage of their project. Given all of the writing that's gone on in the preliminary steps, it's difficult to pinpoint the moment at which these first steps end and "real" writing begins. For short writing projects, the preliminary steps may take only a few minutes and result in little more than a brief outline. For complicated projects, prewriting may take months.

At some point the writer begins writing with some sense of permanence. For the first time in the project, he pays more careful attention to grammar and style. He takes pains to make each sentence follow logically on the last and to make each paragraph treat a single topic. While none of the writing produced at this point is set in stone, the writer crafts each sentence as though it may appear in the finished work.

Once the writer has produced a reasonably complete draft of his work, he is ready to review and revise the draft he's written. There are techniques that help the writer review his own work. In *reverse outlining*, for instance, the writer reads back over what he's written and creates an outline indicating the most important topics of each section and paragraph. This process helps the reader tell, for instance, whether he's put every topic in its proper place, and whether he's treated every topic with the detail it deserves.

However, at this stage it's best to enlist the aid of another reader. Every piece of writing is made to be read, after all, and a piece of writing fails if another reader finds it confusing or unclear. Much of Chapter Three is devoted to a more thorough consideration of reviewing and responding to students' writing and to structuring peer review.

With a reviewer's feedback in hand, the writer is ready to revise the first draft of his work. This stage of the writing process can be a very painful one, involving considerable work and sacrifice. Just as meaningful review of a piece of writing involves attention to more than superficial details like grammar and spelling, meaningful revision often involves significant reworking. Whole sentences, paragraphs, or sections (even well written ones!) may need to be rearranged or eliminated altogether. Moreover, the writer may find it necessary to revise his work several times, each time seeking feedback from a different reviewer, before the work is deemed done.

Most students are not used to performing this sort of deep revision and must be coached to do so effectively. Most students, at first, will revise by making minor adjustments. They will correct any grammatical mistakes that have been pointed out to them. They will reword, often only slightly, phrases they've been told are awkward or confusing. Students resist more substantial rewriting, not only because they're afraid of the work involved but also because they're used to thinking that they're "done" writing once they've finished the first draft. Why go further?

You can counter students' resistance by responding to their work in ways that challenge them to see how the work may be made more clear and more complete. Rather than focusing on grammar (and pointing out, one by one, every error that you find), your responses can show students where their work becomes confusing, and where it is you have questions about it. Responding in this fashion forces students to revise their work to address more meaningful concerns.

Revision Versus Reiteration

For some genres revision is often not feasible. In fact, in a few specific cases, revising one's work is frowned upon or even considered unethical. For instance, in the interest of transparency it would be inappropriate for a student to revise the lab notes he produced while completing an experiment in a chemistry lab. Jeffrey Jablonski and Irwin Weiser encourage a conversation about this scenario in their essay "Raising the Gates of Chem. 110," which appears in Chris M. Anson's (ed.) *The WAC Casebook* (2002).

However, multiple iterations of the same genre offer students an opportunity akin to revision. Certain genres, such as lab reports, mathematical proofs, and blocks of computer language pseudocode, are strongly typified by easily identifiable salient characteristics. Even if students are not asked to revise a single instance of such a genre, your response to their writing can guide them in recognizing these characteristics. The next time they write in that genre, their writing will benefit from this recognition.

For example, a mathematical proof should state the method of proof to be attempted. It should include words indicating logical causality and transition (for example *thus, therefore, because, or since*). It should make explicit mention of hypotheses (that which is known) and conclusions (that which is to be shown). Stylistically, it should be clear and direct, and as succinct as possible without sacrificing clarity and directness. In a typical "Introduction to Proofs" course, a student may be asked to write more than a hundred proofs during the course of a single semester, and it is impossible to ask a student to revise every single proof she writes. However, by reading the instructor's responses to each of her proofs the student gains a better understanding of what makes a "good" proof. As she sets about writing her next proof, the student can use this understanding to craft a better proof than those she has written before.

Reinforcing and Reflecting on the Writing Process

Since most students in quantitative fields are relatively reluctant writers, it is unlikely that many of them have given much thought to the process I've laid out. However, if they are asked to attend to this process and apply it consistently, their writing will improve. Moreover, the more familiar with the process your students become, the more they will be able to get out of it when they use it. Thus we do well to reinforce the process and encourage the students to reflect on it as they grow more comfortable using it.

No two students will engage the writing process in precisely the same way, and once your students have applied each step of the process a few times in their work, they'll begin to recognize their personal approaches to completing those steps. You can strengthen this recognition by asking students to write informally on a simple prompt like "Describe what the writing process looks like to *you*." The self-awareness the students gain through this reflection will help them more readily apply the writing process in the future. Moreover, if students are asked to share their reflections with each other, they can compare their personal processes and learn new ways of making those processes more effective.

Five or six weeks into the spring 2009 semester, I had students in my proofs course perform such a reflection on their proof-writing process. Many students had yet to establish a regular writing process, but several had, and they gave very clear pictures of their personal processes. Salem Johnston, one of the class's strongest students, offered an excellent model to her peers (see the textbox).

ONE STUDENT'S REFLECTION ON HER PROOF-WRITING PROCESS

A. I read the problems the day I get them or soon thereafter. I usually have to read them a lot of times before I even understand what is going on in them. But half the battle is knowing what's going on, so I try to get that done as soon as I can. I look for words I've heard before and think about whether I've seen anything similar. I usually write a "translation" to the side of the problem, something that helps me remember what the problem is asking when I go back to it later.

B. I scrawl. I write ideas down, even if they're stupid (and they probably are at first) or messy. They are usually very unorganized. I scrawl all over the homework paper and when I run out of room there, I scrawl all over notebook paper. This is just to get my ideas out, and if I don't have any ideas, I write out definitions that might be relevant, or really anything at all that might be relevant. For example, if the problem is to show two sets are equal, I write down what I know has to be shown for that to be true: containment in both directions. Just by writing that down and seeing it, I might think of the next step. For that matter, sometimes I just write down the entire problem in my own words.

C. I organize my scrawlings. Still on notebook paper, I write the problems out in order and compile all the ideas I had for each problem into one place. The answers might not be complete, but the ideas are at least organized.

D. I get frustrated and leave it alone for a while. Depending on how much time is left, I stop thinking about it for a few hours or a day so I don't burn out. These homeworks are really hard and if I think about it too much all at once I start getting mad and thinking "When am I ever gonna use this stuff???" Not productive. I take a break and do something completely different.

E. I come back fresh. I take my organized scrawlings to the math lab and crank it out. If no ideas ever came, I ask whoever is around if any ideas ever came to them, including Patrick, who lives right across the hall from the math lab, conveniently! I write out a dress rehearsal of my homework (the whole thing the way I want it to look LaTeXed [typeset], just on notebook paper).

F. I LaTeX it. I won't lie, this takes me forever. But I'm getting better at it and it comes much much easier than it did at first. I usually copy and paste an old homework into a new document and fill things in. That way, I don't have to start from scratch. LaTeXing it makes it SO much clearer and I can find mistakes more easily.

G. I revel in the beauty that LaTeX spits out. So lovely!

Rather than write about their personal writing processes, you might ask your students to draw them instead, as described in Dunn (2001). This alternative mode of expression can be liberating to students in quantitative fields, many of whom respond more favorably to visual tasks than they do textual ones.

STRUCTURING WRITING ASSIGNMENTS

We can help students engage the writing process at many levels. At the level of the assignment itself, we can provide structure that leads the students naturally from one step of the assignment to the next. This structure becomes clearer still if we lay out explicit learning goals for the writing students will do. At the level of the course, we can schedule our writing assignments so that they increase in challenge and complexity from first to last, helping our students to grow as writers throughout the term. Finally, we can structure our assignments across various courses in our curricula, so that students' instruction in writing flows smoothly from one course to another, taking into account students' intellectual development as they progress in their college careers.

Admittedly, it takes time to put these structures in place. Creating new writing assignments takes time, and arranging these assignments strategically throughout a course or across multiple courses takes even more time. However, every hour put into the careful design of a new assignment will save several when the time comes to respond to the writing students produce for those assignments. We all know how much easier (and more enjoyable) it is to grade our students' strongest work than it is to grade the weakest! Time spent in crafting our assignments is time well spent, indeed.

Shaping a Single Assignment

Perhaps the biggest mistake I made when I first began assigning papers in my calculus courses was asking the students to complete their papers in a single monolithic step. The metaphor of the monolith is an appropriate one here: in telling the students to "write a paper on a mathematical topic of your choosing," it was as if I had asked them to scale a sheer rock face without the aid of any climbing equipment and without any training. I gave them no guidance, no structure, and no opportunity to receive feedback. No doubt most of the students, as beginning writers who had never before been asked to write in a math class, had no idea how to tackle such an assignment. In failing to break my assignment down into a series of manageable stages, I was preventing them from finding the handholds they would need in order to climb the rock wall in front of them. Small wonder that the writing I got in response to my prompt was uniformly weak!

It is likely that few of your students have ever received explicit instruction in writing in your discipline. For this reason they will benefit tremendously from whatever help you give them in following the writing process, at least at first. Any writing assignment more complicated than a brief reflection paper can be made more manageable by being broken down into steps. These steps can correspond to the various stages of the writing process outlined earlier in this chapter: the first step may involve prewriting or outlining, while in the next step students complete a first draft. In subsequent steps students review and revise their work before completing the project as a whole. The work the students do at each step should lead them logically to the next, underscoring the cohesion of the writing process.

A good deal of structure can be provided by the design of the assignment itself and the assignment's prompt. If designed effectively, each stage of the assignment can offer a foothold from which students can reach the assignment's next stage. I have come to think of the crafting of the students' assignment as my own writing assignment. I succeed in this assignment if most of my students are able to get a grip on their assignment and make progress from one stage to the next. If students have trouble making this progress, I may have to go back and revise the assignment for future courses.

Of course, as students become more skilled as writers, they will need less and less assistance. The handholds we give students in advanced courses, or even in later weeks of introductory courses, can be, and should be, placed further apart, as long as students can maintain a grip on the overall structure of the assignment. Although we should not let them fall, we must also give them room to stretch and strengthen their skills.

Make Your Learning Outcomes Clear

To write convincingly, students need to know why it is they are writing. At the outset of every writing assignment you should make clear the learning outcomes you hope your students will achieve by completing the assignment. Not only will these outcomes help students focus their writing, they will also help you recognize whether or not the assignment you've designed is helping students in the way you want it to. For instance, if you've indicated that the assignment is meant to help students understand how a scholar in your field structures a grant proposal, yet the assignment gives no indication of that structure, you'll know that you may have to redesign the assignment.

Some outcomes may concern the students' writing itself:

- "This assignment will help you learn to communicate concepts from physical chemistry more clearly."
- "This assignment will give you practice in critiquing others' writing and in responding to that writing with meaningful feedback."

- "This assignment will help you understand the structure of an academic article in computer science."

Other learning outcomes may concern broader course concepts:

- "Completing this consultant's report will help you better understand pricing models."

- "The dialogue you write will allow you to see the advantages and disadvantages of various sampling methods."

- "In writing your 'textbook' chapter you will come to understand the differences between the various methods of mathematical proof."

No matter what outcomes you have, these outcomes should be articulated explicitly. You should also be prepared to discuss these outcomes with your students before they begin their work. This discussion will help students determine both the audience for whom they are writing and the style and tone of the writing they will produce. All of this will help students craft better and more easily readable prose.

Help Students Get Started

Your students will find it easier to begin their work if they are given explicit direction at the initial stage of the assignment. You may require students to apply a specific prewriting strategy and submit whatever writing results from this strategy. You may instead ask for an outline or some other piece of preliminary writing related to the finished piece the students will later produce. The initial stage of the assignment can take many forms, depending on the nature of the overall assignment. The following examples are a representative few; for other inventive ideas, see Axelrod and Cooper (2010); Bean (1996); Gottschalk and Hjortshoj (2004); or Peterson (1996).

Required Prewriting   Given the numerous benefits that accrue from informal preliminary writing, you may wish to require students to perform such writing and submit artifacts of this work, like concept maps or outlines. Since this writing is not meant to be fully formed, you shouldn't hold the students to the same standards by which you'd judge their finished writing. Rather, students should receive a passing grade on this step of the assignment as long as they complete the step.

Indeed, students need not even submit the writing they do at this stage. If you take ten minutes in class to lead the students in a freewrite or a cubing exercise, you can be sure that every student takes part without having to read a word of what they've written. I often begin complex written assignments with just this sort of in-class activity.

Annotated Bibliographies   As I indicated earlier, annotated bibliographies help students makes sense of the sources they've found in their research. For instance, students in our department's senior seminar begin their semester's work by writing an annotated bibliography. After choosing three tentative topics for their research, they seek out at least five sources for each topic, analyzing these sources in a single document. They are asked to summarize each source in a few sentences and to indicate briefly the most pertinent information they've obtained from each source.

I have found that the students view annotated bibliographies as they might a difficult physical regimen: though it is difficult for them to write in this relatively unfamiliar genre, they come to realize the exercise's benefits during the later stages of the project of which it is a part. When asked about the exercise, one student, who has also done undergraduate research outside of the seminar course, said, "I think it's important to know how to summarize ideas about math topics because that's what you do when you do research." Another student was more specific about the benefits he received from writing the bibliography: "Honestly I feel like it was just as useful as the final assignment as it gave me a chance to get you to comment on the information and potential topics I had set forth. A good morale builder that I'm moving in the right direction if nothing else. I feel like it is very helpful to have to think about the assignment beforehand and be forced to consider some topics right at the start as well."

Nearly every student I've ever asked about the assignment expressed similar feelings.

Proposals   As professional writers in our disciplines, we are often asked to write proposals for lengthier written projects such as papers, studies, book chapters, and books. These proposals give us our chance to lay out a basic plan for our projects as we begin to assemble and organize our thoughts. Feedback on our proposals often leads us to envision our projects more clearly and to discover new angles and new ideas.

If writing proposals offers us such a fruitful opportunity, why not offer our students the same opportunity? You might require your students to complete an expository paper on a topic from the area your course treats but leave it up to each student to propose the topic she will write about. In this case a student's proposal will offer one or more potential topics, indicating the reasons she wishes to write about those topics. She may be asked to include an initial survey of the literature, if appropriate. You can respond to students' proposals by suggesting ways to narrow or broaden the topics they have suggested, indicating (as would our own proposals' reviewers) potential obstacles or difficulties.

Sample Prompt 1 (for a Mathematical Economics Course)

For your final writing project you must select a real-world market and apply the methods from our course to analyze that market's behavior. The first step of this project is to write a proposal indicating which market you would like to analyze. Your proposal should describe briefly why the market you propose to analyze is worth analyzing and why you feel you will be able to apply our course's methods to this market successfully. Please back up your claims with specific evidence.

You might instead require that students write on a particular topic but leave it to the individual students to propose a stance they will take on that topic. In your response to each proposal you can help the student to focus her arguments by casting yourself as a rival with an opposing view on the topic.

Sample Prompt 2 (for a Statistical Methods Course)

In your next research project you will analyze the factors that most strongly affect a student's likelihood to cheat on a take-home exam. To begin, write a proposal in which you indicate the factors you think will have the greatest impact in such an analysis. Describe carefully your reasons for choosing these factors.

Finally, you might require students to propose a structure for the later stages of the assignment itself. This sort of proposal is called for when the assignment as a whole is particularly complicated. For example, if students are asked to craft a "textbook" for the course, you might ask them to propose both the list of topics each chapter of their book will address and the way those chapters will be organized to make up the book as a whole. The students' proposals may include rationale for their proposed organization.

Sample Prompt 3 (for a First-Year Physics Course)

We have now completed our discussion of electromagnetism and are ready to begin writing a "textbook chapter" that will treat this area. For our next class, bring a proposal in which you list the topics this chapter must include. Your proposal should include a brief discussion of the ways these topics will be arranged in the chapter, including your rationale for this arrangement.

As we will see later, still more nontraditional assignments may ask students to demonstrate their understanding of your discipline's ideas using expressive genres like short stories, poems, and plays. You might begin such an assignment by asking each student to propose the genre in which she will write to complete the project.

Build In Review and Revision

The only way to ensure that every student will complete more than one draft of a lengthy assignment is to require those drafts by building them into the assignment itself. Indicate specifically the days on which students are to submit drafts and the days on which those drafts will be reviewed.

For particularly lengthy projects, you can ask the students to check in at several different stages of the project. For instance, you might require students to submit first an outline for the project as a whole, then a full introduction and a sketch of the remaining sections, and finally a rough draft of the entire assignment. This is the tack I take with the students in our department's senior seminar, for whom the writing schedule is something like the following:

- Third week of class: Annotated bibliography due
- Seventh week: Rough draft of paper due
- Eighth week: In-class peer review
- Tenth week: Paper abstract due
- Thirteenth week: Final draft of paper due

No matter what you are asking for at any given point during the project, make your expectations clear. For instance, students in our senior seminar are told that their rough drafts need not include complete versions of every section. However, at this point students are asked to indicate the structure of any incomplete section by including a few sentences indicating the directions in which the section will grow.

Finally, be sure also to build in points at which your students will receive feedback. For instance, you might plan on responding to your students' outlines yourself and plan to use class time in the following week to guide the students in a peer review of completed rough drafts. Giving your students multiple checkpoints ensures that they will begin their work sooner and keep a good pace as they move steadily toward completing their assignments.

SEQUENCING ASSIGNMENTS THROUGHOUT A COURSE

As your students make progress in your course, they will gain both the competence and the confidence needed to complete increasingly sophisticated exercises regarding the course's content. You can take these gains into account by sequencing your writing assignments appropriately, with simple exercises at the outset of the term and more involved projects later on. In a way this progression from simple assignments to complex ones mirrors the progression we saw in the process of writing in a single assignment, from early exploratory prewriting to a formalized final draft. In other words, the structure of writing over an entire course may also bear traces of the writing process.

There are other parallels as well. Just as every assignment is designed to help students meet certain learning outcomes, so is every course. It is helpful to come up with a short list of learning outcomes you hope your students will achieve through writing in your course and share these with your students early on. Likely some of your outcomes will be easier to meet and will logically lead into others: "After doing X, students should be able to do Y rather easily." With these learning outcomes in mind, you will find it easier to sequence assignments appropriately, and your students will get more out of the assignments, knowing why they are completing them. L. Dee Fink's *Creating Significant Learning Experiences: An Integrated Approach to Designing College Courses* (2003) contains some excellent guidelines on coming up with course learning outcomes.

For instance, in my first-semester calculus courses, two of the learning goals I include on my syllabus are "Be able to explain to a peer the concepts of *limit, continuity,* and *derivative*" and "Be able to perform and properly interpret derivatives." The first of these goals clearly precedes the second, so I start with the first. To help students learn how to communicate mathematical ideas fluently,

I ask them to write mock dialogues in which they offer their friends intuitive descriptions of technical terms. Once students have gained some confidence in using basic technical terms, I ask them to use the terms in a nontrivial setting. At this point, for example, I can assign a more involved writing exercise in which students must show they can apply derivatives to solve a nontrivial problem in physics or economics.

The exercises in this example are only loosely related: completing the first readies students for the second but does not lead directly into it. However, the structuring of writing assignments can be made more explicit still, with one assignment expressly designed to prepare students to complete the next. This is the case in our department's senior seminar for mathematics majors. Each student in this course first completes an annotated bibliography that helps him evaluate the sources he has uncovered in his initial literature review. This done, he writes a first draft of the traditional expository paper on the topic he's chosen. After this draft is complete, the student finds it easier to put together his final written project, a multimedia presentation on his topic. Every writing assignment in the course builds explicitly on the last.

You can help students to recognize explicitly the evolution of writing throughout a course by requiring them to assemble portfolios that include representative pieces of their writing. In putting together their portfolios, students are challenged to reflect on the ways each piece they've written fits with every other. In an effective portfolio, a student will demonstrate an understanding both of the purpose of each assignment she has completed and of her own success in achieving that purpose. In this way portfolios can help you assess students' achievement of certain skills or course learning outcomes. If those outcomes are identified in advance, portfolios can be an excellent means of assessing students' academic growth during a particular course.

SEQUENCING WRITING FROM COURSE TO COURSE

We take for granted that our students will grow to be more proficient practitioners of our disciplines as they progress in their college careers. We expect our students to gain both competence and confidence from each course they take, and we sequence our courses so that earlier courses prepare them for later ones. I would not dream of asking my first-year students to enroll in a senior-level course on abstract algebra, and my senior math majors would simply be bored in a calculus course.

Similarly, we must recognize also that our first-year students' writing skills are much less well developed than those of our seniors, and plan accordingly. Generally speaking, writers in elementary courses will require more explicit guidance than their more experienced counterparts. They will need more assistance at every stage of the writing process and more models of both good and bad writing. We do well to limit the length and complexity of the writing we assign to students in elementary courses or at least to break those assignments into manageable pieces. As students become more accomplished writers, they will be ready to face more challenging writing assignments.

Coordinating writing from course to course presents administrative challenges as well as pedagogical ones. In any department with more than a few faculty members, coordinating expectations for writing from one course to the next can be difficult. This coordination is especially difficult in departments in which each course is taught regularly by different faculty members with different syllabi. It is more difficult still in disciplines that require students to complete courses in multiple departments.

However, we owe it to our students to do all we can to provide them with a cohesive learning experience from each course to the next. Coordinating writing across several disciplinary courses is a worthwhile goal, and we can meet that goal more easily by establishing departmental learning outcomes for writing. Just as identifying learning outcomes for individual assignments gives those assignments meaning and purpose, and just as identifying such outcomes for individual courses gives structure to the writing in those courses, departmental learning outcomes can help you and your colleagues determine how best to implement writing across your department's curriculum. For each outcome developed, you can identify the courses in which students will naturally achieve that outcome, ensuring that every outcome is addressed with appropriate coursework.

The mathematics department at North Carolina State University (NCSU) gives us an excellent example of how this can be done. The faculty in that department developed a short list of outcomes for both writing and speaking. (These outcomes are further elaborated on the NCSU website at www.chass .ncsu.edu/CWSP/docs/Math_out.pdf.)

NCSU Department of Mathematics Writing and Speaking Outcomes

Students should demonstrate the ability to

1. Read, understand, and make informed judgments about mathematical arguments

2. Generate clearly reasoned, convincing proofs

3. Apply mathematics and mathematical reasoning to solving real-world problems

4. Explain mathematics intelligibly to a variety of audiences

The members of the NCSU math department have structured the departmental curriculum accordingly. For example, the writing assignments students complete in the course titled "Foundations of Advanced Mathematics," which introduces students to rigorous mathematical proofs, are designed to address outcomes 1, 2, and 4. Students then encounter more challenging writing assignments in upper-level courses like "Introduction to Modern Algebra for Mathematics Majors" and "Mathematical Analysis I." These assignments further students' achievement of the same learning outcomes. Students meet outcome 3 through the writing assignments given in more applied mathematics courses like "Computational Mathematics: Models, Methods, and Analysis" and "Introduction to Numerical Analysis I."

This careful structuring of outcomes and courses assists students in their development as writers, but it can do a great deal more. Clearly articulated outcomes and means to measure achievement of those outcomes help faculty identify the roles writing plays in their program of study. They help faculty recognize the ways writing-related outcomes fit into a department's broader curricular goals. They help faculty design orderly program assessment. You can read more about the way these issues interrelate in Anson (2009); Anson and Dannels (2009); Carter (2007); and Carter, Anson, and Miller (2003).

I hope that this chapter has given you a sense of the ways writing takes shape within a single writing assignment, from one assignment to the next, and even from course to course. Although there is no *one* right way to complete a given piece of writing, certain steps occur often enough to make them into a process that can help to guide the writer in a wide variety of writing tasks. Almost invariably the writer moves from informal writing to outlining and organizing, and from here to fleshing out a final draft, maybe after one or more revisions. This trend of increasing elaboration and complexity is evident in courses in which assignments are sequenced in order to give students growing challenges to test their growing skills.

The next question I address concerns our response to the writing our students do. In responding to student writing, there are two fundamental issues we must address. First, we must come up with reasonable ways of assessing the quality of students' writing. Second, we must learn to give students the feedback they will need in order to grow as writers. These are the issues with which Chapter Three deals.

Assessing and Responding to Student Writing

While clearing out a box in my office just a few months ago I came across an interesting artifact of my teaching from many years back. At the bottom of the box was a short stack of papers I'd assigned to a calculus class I was teaching as a graduate student. The papers were written in response to one of the directionless "Write a paper on a mathematical topic of your choice" prompts I'd employed in my earliest attempts at assigning writing. As I mentioned in the Preface, the students' writing was uniformly weak, likely in part due to the fact that I'd not known to guide the students through the writing process.

Most interesting to me was the fact that the papers I'd found said as much about my responses to the students' writing as they did about the writing itself. Every one of the pages I found bled heavily with my red ink. I'd commented critically on nearly everything the students had written. I'd corrected misspellings and noun-verb agreements, I'd added commas and changed some commas to semicolons, and I'd suggested new words and new wording. Hardly a single slip escaped unmarked. Seeing all the red made me remember how frustrated I'd been with the poor quality of the students' writing and how much time I'd spent agonizingly responding to that writing.

I suspect that our reluctance about responding to writing, more than any-thing else, is what keeps many of us in quantitative disciplines from assigning that writing in the first place. "I'm not a trained writer," any one of us might say. "I can't catch all my students' mistakes. How can I be expected to respond to their work?" Moreover, responding to writing takes time. Though the nightmare scenario from my early years of teaching writing may be a worst case, none of us can eye a stack of papers two inches thick without feeling a sinking feeling in our stomachs.

However, assessing and responding to student writing does not need to be such a heinous chore. As I explain in this chapter, you don't have to address every last grammatical or syntactical mistake your students make; in fact, there are good reasons for you not to do this. You don't need detailed knowledge of English composition to assess your students' writing; you only need knowl-edge of your own discipline. Furthermore, responding to writing need not take as much time as you might think. Several of the methods of response I men-tion in this chapter are designed in part to save you from spending hours on a single student's assignment. There are effective, and pedagogically potent, ways to enlist your students' aid in responding to their own writing. Finally, as with every other aspect of teaching writing in the disciplines, no one is better quali-fied than you are to respond to writing in your own discipline. If you're not going to do it, who else can?

I don't mean to say that assessing writing will be effortless. You'll need prac-tice to respond effectively and efficiently to your students' writing, and no mat-ter how skilled at it you become you will still find yourself at a loss when dealing with extraordinarily obstinate writers. Moreover, responding well to writing does take some time, though the time you spend in composing your responses can be reduced dramatically by responding in the right way at the right time. In the end, offering students meaningful responses to their writing is well worth the time it takes.

My aim in this chapter is to guide you through the basics of assessing and responding to student writing. Throughout this chapter, as elsewhere in this book, I use the word *writing* to stand for more than the finished written pro-duct. Keep in mind that writing is something that is done, not something that is made. If we value writing as a process we owe it to our students to assess and to respond to all aspects of the process. That is, we can, and should, offer our stu-dents guidance at many different stages in their writing.

Moreover, there are really two tasks we must complete when we respond to student writing. First, we must come up with a meaningful way of measuring the quality of our students' written work at each stage of its development. To do this we have to come with some criteria that address not only aspects of composition in general (for example, clarity, tone, diction, purpose, and audience) but also aspects peculiar to our individual disciplines. For instance, given the central role that numerical and logical correctness play in many quantitative fields, to what extent should these aspects of a student's writing influence our assessment of the quality of that writing?

Second, we must come up with ways to offer our students the direction they need to grow as writers. To help meet this goal, our responses to our students' writing should include "formative" feedback in addition to "summative" feedback. That is, our responses should do more than tell students how well they've *done*; our responses should also tell students how well they're *doing*, and how they can adjust their writing in order to make it clearer, more complete, and more correct as their written work takes shape.

I spend the first part of this chapter introducing some basic criteria you may wish to keep in mind when assessing writing. Given the wide variety of writing we might assign, no single set of criteria, and no single rubric or style sheet, will apply equally well in every setting. The best we can do here is to lay out some general measures that might help you to design your own. I then turn to the issue of responding to student writing. I touch on two means of responding: in writing (on students' written work or on completed rubrics that will be returned to them) and in face-to-face conferencing. I highlight several techniques that will help you make your responses helpful to your students and that will not take too much of your time. Finally, I describe ways to help your students engage in peer review. I give some tips on structuring peer review in your classroom and some ideas for encouraging ongoing peer review outside of class. All of these activities help to save time and effort by freeing you from having to read every last draft of students' written work and are applicable in a wide variety of courses and disciplines.

RECOGNIZING GOOD WRITING

Few of us have any trouble recognizing good writing when we see it, particularly writing in fields closely related to our own. After reading a paragraph of each we notice the difference in quality between an article from, say, *Scientific American* or *Nature* and a paper written by a typical first-year chemistry student. Pinning down precisely where that difference lies may be more difficult, for it might take us some time to identify the criteria we're applying in our unconscious analysis.

What is it about the former piece that distinguishes it as the superior written work? It's likely that the former piece is clearer and more well composed. Its writer likely has a stronger sense of purpose and audience and a firmer grasp of the stylistic conventions of her genre. Other, more discipline-specific criteria may come into play in our assessment. For many of us it takes time to identify these criteria because we were never taught them explicitly. Rather, we learned how to recognize good writing in our disciplines by apprenticing with our own professors and advisers.

These criteria differ from one discipline to the next, and the criteria vary tremendously depending on the kind of writing being assessed. It's not hard to find expert advice on assessing the quality of the more traditional disciplinary genres like journal articles, technical reports, and so forth. For instance, Gerver (2007) and Krantz (1997) offer direction in assessing formal mathematics writing, and Zobel (2004) addresses writing in computer science. Sorby and Bulleit (2006) look at writing in engineering; McCloskey (2000) takes on economics; and Alley (1996) and O'Connor (1991) take a look at science writing in general. Clearly there is no shortage of technical style guides and how-to manuals detailing the drafting of these traditional genres. (For a list of similar resources, see the Readings and Resources at the end of Chapter One and the Recommended Readings and Resources at the end of the book.)

However, we cannot focus our attention solely on traditional types of academic writing. There are no limits to the diversity of writing assignments we can ask our students to complete in our courses. Many of these genres are far removed from the kinds of writing treated by the sources I've listed. For this reason it will be helpful for us to take a step back from the specific guidelines the sources offer and develop yet more basic criteria that will help us recognize good writing in any context.

For the past several years I've based my writing assessment on what I call the "Four Cs": clarity, composition, completeness, and correctness. I'll say a few words about each of these criteria. Each is broad enough and flexible enough to allow reinterpretation from assignment to assignment and from course to course. The boundaries among these criteria are often blurry, but each addresses some aspects of writing the others do not. Taken as a whole, and appropriately adapted for each assignment, they serve to capture nearly every facet of writing my students perform.

I don't mean these criteria to be ready-made means to assess student writing. Rather, I mean them to help you think about the aspects of your students' writing you're most interested in measuring. Keeping in mind your own course learning goals, you should be able to come up with a few criteria that are most meaningful and useful to you.

Clarity

There's a great deal tied up in the clarity of a piece of writing. For instance, writing clearly requires attention to audience. To write clearly the writer must be aware of her readers' depth of understanding and their familiarity with terminology and notation. Any terminology and notation the writer uses should be defined carefully and used consistently. Many beginning writers have trouble identifying their audience and struggle when trying to take control of terminology. When they use technical terms they don't fully understand, their work can come off sounding stilted or "jargony." It can sound as though the writer's writing to impress, and not to inform.

Clear writing also requires attention to the structure of the writing. This structure must make the purpose of the writing clear, through strategic placement of important ideas and well-organized arguments. In this regard it's sometimes hard to differentiate between clarity and composition.

Composition

This criterion takes into account the flow of the writing and its overall cohesiveness. Well-composed writing will flow smoothly and be easy, and pleasant, to read. Composition can be measured on a small scale, word by word and sentence by sentence. It can also be measured on a large scale, taking into account the structure of the piece of writing as a whole.

On the small scale, we can ask how well the writer's words are arranged into sentences, and sentences into paragraphs. Each sentence should be easy to read and free of unnecessary flourishes. Active phrasing is stronger than passive phrasing, and active phrasing gives agency to the writer. Each paragraph should treat a single topic. That topic should be made clear at the paragraph's outset and further developed and supported throughout the remainder of the paragraph.

On the large scale, we can ask how well the writer puts his paragraphs together to help him develop his argument. Are the transitions from one paragraph to the next smooth? These transitions can be aided by signal phrases that direct the reader from one part of the writing to the next. "As we mentioned in the last paragraph" reminds the reader of what's just been said; "we will soon see that" tells the reader to keep a thought in mind, for it will soon be relevant once again. Phrases like these are extremely important in writing in the quantitative disciplines, given how well they help the reader follow the writer's logic.

Completeness

A piece of writing can be clear and well composed yet still not tell the whole story. Thorough arguments are desirable in any discipline, and one person's theories will likely get a warmer reception than another's if the former are more complete or offer a better explanation of known facts. However, completeness is even more crucial in many quantitative fields, where an incomplete argument or explanation is not only inferior, it's invalid.

For instance, consider a mathematical proof. In constructing a proof, the writer assumes some set of hypotheses and from them deduces the desired conclusion by applying accepted logical arguments. Often the hypotheses require the writer to consider several cases. For the proof to be deemed complete, the writer must address every single case that can arise, and she must be sure there are no gaps in her argument. A proof that does not do this is simply not a proof at all; it is incomplete. The same can be said of computer programs, derivations of physical laws, and explanations of chemical principles, in each of which every eventuality must be handled.

Correctness

Correctness, like completeness, has a place in every kind of academic writing. Tenable claims, offered with strong evidence and convincing arguments, are always highly prized. This is the case even in fields like literature, where objective certainty is not always given. For instance, two students may offer two very different interpretations of the same short story, the interpretations depending on the students' individual upbringings and experiences. It is possible for these interpretations to be equally valid, and to some extent the validity of each rests on the quality of the argument the student puts forward in support of it.

However, in the quantitative disciplines we encounter objective correctness more frequently than elsewhere. In these disciplines we often find that there is a single correct answer to a given problem, and the validity of our argument or exposition suffers if that answer is not obtained. Therefore we cannot simply set aside correctness when we assess our students' writing.

How much weight should we give correctness? Clearly this weight will vary from assignment to assignment. For assignments meant to help students develop strong communication skills, correctness need not weigh as heavily as it might for assignments in which students must perform numerous measurements, proofs, or computations. Moreover, there are varying degrees of correctness: some errors are clearly more costly than others. When a student misplaces a minus sign or incorrectly expands a binomial, his mistake is less critical than when he consistently misapplies fundamental physical principles.

Let Your Students Help Generate Assessment Criteria

Whatever criteria for good writing you come up with, it's important to let your students know these criteria early on, before they write a single word. Not only does this give them a fair chance to know the way their work will be weighed; it will also help them craft that work in the first place. If they know in advance what qualities you expect to find in their writing, students will take greater efforts to meet your expectations.

You can do more than this: you can let your students help you come up with your assessment criteria. After all, while it's easier to follow the rules if you know what the rules are ahead of time, it's easier still to follow the rules if you had a hand in making them up. Asking your students to design their own criteria gives them a strong sense of agency and authorship. This exercise isn't as dangerous as you might think: in my experience students are quite adept at recognizing the qualities that make good writing good. Though they may not express them as smoothly or as succinctly as I might, the criteria my students come up with on their own seldom differ significantly from those I've come up with myself. I'll have more to say about this issue when I introduce the "Good Writing/Bad Writing" exercise later in the chapter. For now, I address the ways we can offer students guidance in our responses to their writing.

GIVING GUIDANCE IN REVISION

Meaningful revision is deep. As we know well from our experience as professional writers in our disciplines, there is often little resemblance between the initial draft of a written work and the final version that we produce often weeks, months, or even years after the writing process began. Significant changes occur to the work during the writing process. We make these changes in response to feedback from others or simply to reflect shifts in our own thoughts. As new ideas come to mind, we may add or take away entire sections, or we may simply rearrange sections that were there in the first place. We may develop, tweak, and toy with transitions from one part of the work to another, playing with them until they work together smoothly. By the time we are done, the structure of the written work as a whole may be appreciably altered.

Most of us did not learn to revise in this manner without some instruction, and our students will require the same instruction. Unless led to do otherwise, our students are likely to revise their work only superficially. They will focus their attention on correcting whatever grammatical and syntactical mistakes we point out to them. If we say nothing about it, they will likely be satisfied with the overall structure of their work and will ignore deeper issues like clarity, composition, and argument.

Therefore, it is our job to shift our students' attention from the surface of their writing to its deeper aspects. We can do this in several ways. We can minimize the attention we pay to superficial elements such as grammar and punctuation. We can challenge students to puzzle out the problems in their own writing by asking probing questions. We can respond as honest readers, indicating where our understanding breaks down as we read their work. Finally, we can demonstrate to our students that revision is simply a part of the process, and that even practiced writers have to engage in it.

Fortunately, all of these response methods take far less time to perform than punctiliously pointing out every mistake students make in their writing. Moreover, if you give students more careful guidance in the earlier stages of their writing (on first drafts, for instance), they will need less guidance in the later stages, saving you the time of giving complicated feedback later on in the semester, when you're sure to be busier with other things. In any case, it makes sense to respond more fully to students' writing in the earlier stages, for it is in these stages they can still make changes to their work. No matter how detailed the feedback you give a student on the final draft of her paper, it serves no purpose, for at that point she'll have no further opportunity to act on the feedback you give.

Put the Pen Down

Many of us are reluctant to assign much writing in our courses for fear that responding to this writing will prove too time consuming. Moreover, some of us worry that our own grasp of grammar is too weak to qualify us as teachers of writing. "How can I expect to train my students to use commas correctly if I'm not even sure how to use them correctly myself?"

Fortunately, the literature on responding to writing suggests that emphasis on superficial issues like spelling and grammar can be detrimental to students' development as stronger writers (for example, see Lindemann, 1995; Beach & Friedrich, 2006). If we point out every grammatical misstep our students make, they are likely to respond by correcting only the mistakes we have indicated. As Nancy Sommers (1982) points out, this trains our students to think of revision as little more than proofreading. On the other hand, if we focus our attention on the more critical shortcomings of their writing, our students are likely to respond by performing deeper and more thorough revision. These observations suggest that whatever comments we write on students' papers should not concern their comma splices and run-on sentences but rather the gaps in their logic and the errors in their arguments.

The first time you read each student's work, do so without a pen in your hand. Read the work to comprehend it and not correct it. For most writing this initial reading will go very quickly; I find that I can read a typical five-page paper in two or three minutes. After reading all of the students' work this way, read through each piece of writing once more, making comments only at the places where the writing confused you or made you wish it were clearer. Your comments there can be brief ones; you can wait until the end of the work to offer more thorough feedback.

In your end notes, elaborate on the primary problems you found in the student's work. Don't tell a student that her writing is satisfactory if it's not. Make it clear, when necessary, that you expect her to perform significant revision. Be critical, but don't overdo it. Even if a student's writing shows numerous weaknesses, it is best to focus on a small number of them at a time: any writer will get overwhelmed when asked to take on too many tasks when revising. It's also important to point out a few things that the student has done well. This will give the student encouragement, and it will also give her something to hold on to and focus as she undertakes revision. You can find more about writing effective end notes in Smith (1997) and Sommers (1982).

Writing end notes takes a bit more time than the initial reading. Depending on the strength of the student's writing, you may spend anywhere from five to fifteen minutes per piece. I find it easiest to ask students to submit their work electronically whenever possible, so that I may respond electronically in turn; it takes me far less time to type my responses than it would to write them by hand. A number of new software applications allow you to record electronic audio notes to include in your responses to students, potentially saving you even more time and allowing you to respond orally, offering more nuanced and subtle feedback to your students on their writing.

What if the student's writing is simply so riddled with grammatical errors that you cannot even make out her argument? One way to deal with this issue is to focus your attention on one or two families of errors, for example, subject-verb disagreement and misplaced modifiers. Correct one or two instances of each family for the student and let her know that you would like her to correct all other instances in her writing before you consider reading it again. Doing this not only saves you the time and trouble of training the student in basic grammatical principles, it also encourages the student to learn to recognize violations of those principles herself.

Haswell (1983) introduced an alternative response technique he called "minimal marking." It is quickly done and it is easy to do, for it places the burden of cleaning up the writing on the student who wrote it in the first place. When using minimal marking you place one or more checkmarks in the margin next to each line in which a superficial error occurs, one checkmark for each error. It is up to the student to identify and correct the error. When you respond in this way you refuse to serve as the student's copyeditor, challenging her to find her own mistakes. This technique works best when you offer the student a chance to conference with you or others about the nature of the errors she's making.

Respond with Questions, and Respond as an Honest Reader

Putting your pen down and using minimal marking help you avoid a common pitfall in responding to student work, namely, being overly prescriptive. It's tempting for us to respond didactically, offering our students specific suggestions for improving their writing. Though some general suggestions can offer much-needed direction, if you're too specific in your suggestions students will be robbed of their chance to explore their own solutions to the problems their writing poses.

Rather than offering suggestions to your students, offer them questions instead. By responding with questions you avoid being prescriptive. Asking a student questions about his writing, as would an honest reader attempting to understand the student's point of view, allows you to indicate places where his logic breaks down, to inquire about missing data or ideas, or to register confusion. Asking questions doesn't fix the broken logic, fill in the missing data, or clear up the writing that's confused you. It's up to the student to do these things as he adjusts his writing in response to your questions. Instead of showing the student how to fix his work, you've challenged him to find a way to fix it himself.

Admittedly, it can be hard for us to respond as the honest readers for whom our students intend to write. We're considerably more knowledgeable about our disciplines than our students are, so it's easy for us to pave over the holes in our students' logic without them having to do it for us. Ideally we should resist the urge to read their writing this way. We should read as though we are coming to the topic afresh, with no more knowledge than our students present us in their work. We should allow ourselves to become confused when a student's writing wanders and to lose our way when that writing is unclear. Challenge the student to understand why it is you are confused and to confront that confusion by adjusting her explanation. After all, it's her task to explain her meaning to you, and should you lose yourself in her arguments it's up to her to help you find your way out.

It might help you to see an example of how this sort of responding can play out in a quantitative classroom. In their article "What's an Assignment Like You Doing in a Course Like This? Writing to Learn Mathematics" (1990) George D. Gopen and David A. Smith apply the critical method known as "reader expectation theory" in responding to their students' writing. As they point out, this theory "was born of the linguistic discovery that readers expect certain components of the *substance* of prose (especially context, action, and emphatic material) to appear in certain well-defined places in the *structure* of the prose" (p. 8; emphasis theirs). Put another way, as readers we expect certain elements of the material we're reading (subjects, objects, and actions, for instance) to appear in certain places, and the effect on us as readers can be jarring if our expectations are not met.

For the first couple weeks of a first-semester calculus course, Gopen and Smith responded to their students' lab reports with questions calling attention to these elements. They then devoted a class period to a peer review session in which they prompted students to ask the same questions of each others' work: "What's happening here? . . . Whose story is this? Who is the agent? What seems to require emphasis within a given sentence? Is it in the stress position?" (p. 16). This activity helped the calculus students use their writing more intentionally. The students' writing became tighter and more precise. Furthermore, their students learned to write with stronger agency, eliminating the passive voice and making themselves the authors of their knowledge.

You can find more on responding as an honest reader in Karen A. Schriver's essay "Revising for Readers: Audience Awareness in the Writing Classroom" (1993). This article is replete with other excellent ideas for coaching revision effectively.

Use a Rubric

For some writing assignments it may be very easy for you to come up with a checklist, a performance list, or a rubric, each of which in some way summarizes the criteria you use to assess students' responses to that assignment. Arter and McTighe (2001) give careful definitions of all of these instruments. Roughly, a checklist merely lists the aspects of a piece of writing you want to be present, leaving space for a "yes/no" response. A performance list permits a bit more flexibility by allotting a certain number of potential points to be scored for each such aspect (for example, 5 points for clarity of purpose, 5 points for computational correctness, and so on). A rubric goes further, describing exactly what each possible score on each possible aspect might look like. An example of a simple rubric I wrote for a final exam essay question in an introductory statistics course taught in my department is given in Table 3.1.

There are some obvious advantages to using a rubric. Foremost among these is the time it will save you in responding to your students' writing. For instance, referring to Table 3.1, it takes only a few seconds to make a mark in the level 3 column for the first row than it does to write, "You make minor mistakes (notational or arithmetic) in your computations." Moreover, for many assignments you may be able to anticipate the difficulties students will face in advance, allowing you to address those difficulties specifically in your rubric. This will save you the time it would have taken to comment specifically about a common problem on several different students' written work.

Furthermore, a well-designed rubric will make it easy for you to convert qualitative feedback into a quantitative score, if this sort of score is needed for purposes of grading. An analytic rubric, on which each criterion is allotted a

Table 3.1

Sample Rubric for an Inferential Statistics Problem in an Introductory Statistics Course

	Not Met		Partially Met	Fully Met
Criterion	**Level 1**	**Level 2**	**Level 3**	**Level 4**
Demonstrated understanding of the mathematical process under-lying inferential statistics	Not understood	Major errors	Minor errors (e.g., in notation or arithmetic)	Correctly completed
Clarity of articulation of the necessary criteria needed to apply inferential statistics	Not clear on the concept	Vaguely understands the criteria	Criteria stated but only in general terms	Criteria clearly stated in context of the problem
Interpretation of the results of the computation	Wrong conclusion reached	Wrong conclusion reached but understands context of problem	Correct conclusion reached but fails to contextualize conclusion	Correct conclusion and clear concluding statement, indicating knowledge of the prob-lem's context

Source: Adapted from University of North Carolina Asheville Department of Mathematics Student Learning Outcomes assessment.

given number of points (as in Table 3.1), makes quantitative scoring very straightforward. Rubrics help you to assign scores more consistently from student to student as well.

Using a rubric does not abrogate the need for you to give students the valuable qualitative feedback on their writing that checkmarks and ratios cannot offer. You should supplement your scoring on the rubric itself with summary remarks much like those you would place at the end of a student's written work. However, this can be done particularly quickly if you keep your rubric online and type your comments rather than writing them. If your handwriting is as bad as mine is, your students will appreciate your typing your comments, too!

You can find much more information on constructing rubrics in Arter and McTighe's *Scoring Rubrics in the Classroom: Using Performance Criteria for Assessing and Improving Student Performance* (2001). Although this text is written with K–12 instructors in mind, much of its content is relevant to college and university faculty as well. Perhaps its greatest strength is its long list of sample rubrics. You can find further examples of disciplinary-specific rubrics in Allen and Tanner (2006); Huba and Freed (2000); Luft (1999); and Lynd-Balta (2006).

Model Good Revision

We learn many things more easily when given good examples of how those things appear or function. Revision is no exception: students benefit tremendously by seeing how revision is performed by others, even if that revision is imperfect. Zimmerman and Kitsantas (2002) demonstrate this convincingly, showing that students learn more readily how to revise their writing when shown models for revision than when asked to revise without the help of models. Notably, they also show that students gain more from observing others struggle with revision tasks than they do from observing flawless revision.

If you can find examples of revision to share with your students, take the time to do this. For a given course, these examples may come from the students in the course itself or from students who have taken the course in the past. If one of your students shows great talent in revising her writing from one draft to the next, ask that student if you can share her work with the class (anonymously, if she prefers) as a model for the revision process.

If you are in a position to share multiple versions of your own writing with your students, then share these versions, if you feel comfortable doing so. Whenever I receive feedback from a referee on a manuscript I've recently submitted, I bring that feedback to class with me and share it with my students. I show the students the reviewer's comments, pointing out where it was in my work that the reviewer took issue with my writing. I ask the students to discuss why they think the reviewer may have felt the way he did and how they think I might best respond to the reviewer's concerns. Later, after I've had a chance to revise my work, I bring it back to class and show my students how I've changed the writing around to address the reviewer's concerns.

Offering students a view of our own and others' processes of revision accomplishes a number of goals. As often as not, the revisions that even the best writers have to make are substantial ones, revisions that address more than typos or grammatical mistakes. Students therefore get a chance to see how a piece of writing may undergo major modification before being deemed complete. Furthermore, by letting students in on others' revision processes we give them authority and expertise, showing them that they might have meaningful things to say, even about very advanced writing in their discipline. Finally, this sharing shows students that nobody's perfect: they are always relieved to see that even those of us who have been writing professionally for many years still don't get it completely right the first time around. In the end, the best thing that can come of modeling good revision is the realization that though revision is an inherently humbling experience, it should not be a humiliating one.

Face-to-Face Conferencing

When responding to student writing, we need not confine our responses to written feedback alone. If you have the opportunity to do so, meeting your students to talk about their writing can help to give them the focus they'll need to complete effective revision. Admittedly, meeting face to face with every one of your students can be time consuming, and it may take a good deal of organizational skill to arrange meetings with every student in all but your smallest classes. (Meeting with several students at once, each of whom has similar issues with her writing, can save time here.)

However, these efforts offer tremendous rewards. Though your written comments can convey a great deal of information, there's simply no substitute for the rich interaction offered by a face-to-face dialogue. A face-to-face meeting with a student gives you the chance to inflect your comments with subtlety and care. Such a meeting also gives the student a chance to reply to your feedback immediately, responding to your comments and questions with comments and questions of his own. This can set up a real-time conversation through which you work together to promote substantive changes in the student's work. Even a fifteen-minute meeting can help give much-needed direction.

To make the most of whatever time you can offer your students, make sure they come ready for their meetings. Your conferences will go much more smoothly if your students have thought in advance about what they'd like to get out of their time with you. They should come ready with questions about their assignments: Is there some aspect of the assignment they're having difficulty grasping? Where in their writing are they having the most difficulty? Which of the written comments you've made on their work are they unable to understand?

Make sure your students know what to expect, and what not to expect, out of your meetings with them. The meetings will give them a chance to talk with you about the overall direction of their writing; they will not be copyediting sessions. You will give them feedback on the organization of their writing, and on its cohesiveness and clarity; you will not proofread it for spelling errors and grammatical correctness. You will help them to learn how they can work to improve their writing; you will not improve the writing for them.

Meeting with a student to talk about his writing in person also gives you the chance to have the student read his work out loud. This simple action accomplishes a number of goals:

- It allows the student to actually hear his words, drawing attention to places where his wording may be clumsy or rough or where his tone may be off.

- It forces the student to unpack the meaning buried in specialized or technical notation. In reading this notation out loud the student must translate it into ordinary words. This serves as a check on his understanding of that notation.

- It challenges the student to slow down. He will read out loud far more slowly than he will read to himself, and the extra time it takes him to do the former helps him catch mistakes he would otherwise miss.

- It adds richness to the words the student has written by involving another sense. This "multimodality" can help the student discover new connections among his ideas.

Some students may be reluctant to read their work out loud. This is understandable, for hearing their words spoken makes students more accountable for those words. Just as you can model revision by showing students your own peers' comments on your own writing, you can put your students at ease about reading out loud by reading your own work out loud to them.

Recently in one of my courses I pointed out that a reviewer had drawn attention to my frequent use of "fluff" words in a piece she'd reviewed, like "in order to" (instead of simply "to") and "that which I had written" (instead of "that I had written"). I read out loud to my students several sentences that contained these phrases. Nearly every student in the room admitted that the fluff-filled sentences sounded stuffy and aloof and that simplifying the wording improved the tone of the writing. They were able to chuckle at my mild self-effacement, and I believe they came away from that class feeling a little less anxious about reading their own work out loud.

Reading out loud is helpful in any meeting about writing, whether it takes place between a student and her instructor or between a student and a tutor, a writing center consultant, or even another student. Reading math-heavy writing out loud may be more than helpful in these latter meetings; it may be essential. After all, tutors, writing center consultants, and students' peers may have difficulty puzzling out mathematical notation as it's written, and this notation may only make sense when the student reads it out loud.

PEER REVIEW

As I mentioned early on in this chapter, every one of us can recognize good writing when we read it. With a bit more effort and training, our students can do this, too. In fact, if they are adequately prepared for the challenges involved in reading quantitative writing, your students can offer each other valuable assistance as they write. Asking your students to assist each other by reviewing their written work helps to meet many goals, all of them important ones. In performing peer review

- Your students develop authority, authorship, and autonomy.
- They become more astute at assessing the quality of writing put before them.
- They obtain useful feedback from members of an audience other than you.
- You are freed from having to respond to every single piece of student writing, saving you a great deal of time and effort.

Of course, many of these benefits accrue most strongly when peer review activities are well planned and well managed, and organizing these activities takes inventiveness and coordination. Effective peer review takes time and practice, and the results will be mixed: inevitably some students offer more substantive feedback than others, even when students are helped to understand what criteria to apply. Furthermore, just as you'll have to overcome students' resistance to writing, you'll also have to overcome their resistance to peer review of that writing. "I don't know how to write . . . and I certainly don't know how to tell someone else how to do it!"

Despite these difficulties, a great deal of research demonstrates that the benefits of peer review are worth the effort it takes to set it up (for example, see Nilson, 2003, and Topping, 1998). The key to making peer review work is to be patient and to prepare students for peer review one step at a time. Ease them into it, and be ready for some reluctance at first. Their initial attempts at peer review will be rough. Give them a good deal of guidance in offering feedback, especially in the beginning. Give them numerous opportunities to perform peer review, so that they have a chance to practice as they grow to depend less and less on the guidance you give them.

Preparing Students for Peer Review

It's important to lay a solid foundation for peer review before you ask students to offer one another feedback on their written work. This preparation is particularly important in our disciplines, where students are often unaccustomed to a great deal of writing. As Linda Nilson puts it, "The problems with student peer feedback seem to boil down to three: the intrusion of students' emotions into the evaluative process, their ignorance of professional expectations and standards for various types of work, and their laziness in studying the work and/or in writing up the feedback. Emotion, ignorance, and laziness are formidable barriers, especially in combination" (2003, p. 35). In contrast, successful peer review requires students to be careful readers who are knowledgeable about the criteria they will be applying to the writing they read. Successful peer review requires them to be willing to ask one another difficult questions and often to make difficult suggestions concerning one another's work. It also requires them to be able to communicate these questions and suggestions respectfully.

Fortunately there are ways you can help students gain competence and confidence in doing these things before they even look at one another's work. Often as early as the first day of class you can assign pre–peer review exercises that are challenging, fun, and relevant to your course material. I give a few examples of such exercises, indicating the roles they play in preparing students to do peer review. You can find other examples of peer review activities in Gragson and Hagen (2010, in chemistry); Parke (2008, in statistics); and Smith, Broughton, and Copley (2006, in economics).

Good Writing/Bad Writing   One of my favorite exercises is one I assign on the second day of my course introducing students to mathematical proofs. The "Good

Writing/Bad Writing" exercise is meant to help students identify the salient characteristics that distinguish good writing from bad. In doing this, students generate their own criteria for assessing one another's writing.

I first give students three short samples of writing in response to a prompt they might find in a more traditionally writing-intensive course, like history or literature. I then ask the students, working in groups of three or four, to rate the quality of the writing samples and to rank them. I ask them to pay careful attention to the criteria they use in establishing their rankings and to write those criteria down. Most of the time students find this an easy task, for they are more astute at recognizing good writing than they think they are.

This done, I then give the students three short mathematical proofs, each purporting to show the truth of the same claim. (The students are sure to be familiar with the claim, for it's the same claim we would have proven on the first day of class, just a day or two earlier.) Again I ask the students to rate the quality of the writing samples, to rank them, and to keep track of the criteria they use in their assessment. Though this stage of the exercise often takes a bit longer than the first, students are often surprised by how easy it is for them to distinguish good "math writing" from bad. They are also surprised at how strongly the criteria they apply to the mathematical writing accord with the criteria they had earlier applied to the nonmathematical writing.

I give the final stage of the exercise as homework for the next day of class. Working in the groups they formed in class, the students are now to write two responses each to two simple prompts, one that is mathematical and one that is not. I ask students to write one response as well as they can and the other as poorly as they can, according to the criteria they've established as a class. The students will share some of their responses with one another in class when we next meet. Of course, the examples of "bad writing" they've come up with are hilarious, but the exercise is as useful as it is fun: they've had a chance to actively apply the criteria they generated, and they're much more ready to use those criteria to assess authentic mathematical writing.

Indeed, the entire exercise is useful and serves several important functions. Students complete it with a list of criteria they can later apply as they are examining their own and others' writing throughout the rest of the semester. Creating this list gives the students a legitimate sense of authorship and authority, more so than if I had simply handed them a list of criteria without involving them in the process of its creation. (Generally the list they generate differs only slightly from my own.) The confidence they gain through this exercise is tremendous, too. They finish the exercise feeling more ready to write and more ready to read.

The exercise is highly relevant to the course material, as well. It offers an excellent counterexample to the claim that disciplinary writing instruction takes away class time that could be devoted to disciplinary course content. This exercise helps students with their writing *while* they are engaging the course content. Moreover, the exercise is readily adaptable to any discipline.

Reviewing Professional Writing   A bit later in the same proofs course, I often assign an exercise to illustrate the universality of the assessment criteria they've developed to help them in their peer review. In the assignment "You Make the Call," students are given passages out of several different textbooks. Each of these passages treats the same mathematical claim, either one we have already proven together as a class or one that students have seen in a prerequisite course.

The students are then asked to take time outside of class to review each passage and to apply our course's writing criteria to each of them. The students write summaries of their reviews, indicating which passages were most successful according to various criteria. They bring their summaries to class and share them with one another and compare their notes, in effect peer reviewing their own reviews. My students rarely fail to be impressed with the amount of detail they are able to discern through close reading of the texts they've been given.

Mark Hoffman, a professor of computer science at Quinnipiac University, uses a similar assignment in his course on operating systems (see Smart, Hudd, Delohery, Pritchett, & Hoffman, 2010). The "Textbook Selection Project" asks students to act as textbook committee members who are considering three different textbooks for use in the course the students are currently enrolled in. In weighing the merits of these three texts, students will decide which text offers the clearest and most complete treatment of the course concepts.

The first part of the exercise is repeated four times during the semester. On each occasion, Hoffman has the students read an excerpt from each of the three texts, all three excerpts treating a single topic. The students must respond in their course reading journals to a series of questions regarding each of the excerpts they've read. The questions (presented in the box) are meant to get the students thinking about clarity of the writing and about the breadth of its coverage. The questions do not have "yes or no" answers; rather, they demand richer answers, forcing students to think more deeply about the reading. Nilson (2003) suggests using such questions to promote close reading.

READING QUESTIONS FOR THE "TEXTBOOK SELECTION PROJECT"

1. Find a sentence in *each* book excerpt that best *summarizes the main idea.* Of the sentences you selected—one from each excerpt—which one is the *clearest*? In 3–5 sentences, tell why you chose this sentence.

2. Identify the key words in each sentence you selected in question 1. If you identify more than three key words, select the *best three key words* for the main idea over all of the book excerpts. In 3–5 sentences, explain why you chose these key words.

3. From *all* the book excerpts, find the one sentence that is *the least clear.* In 3–5 sentences, tell why you chose this sentence.

4. Find one sentence in *one* book excerpt that describes *a topic or idea that does not appear in the others.* In 3–5 sentences, explain why it is critical or not critical to include this topic or idea.

The students then discuss their journal responses in class. "They are opinionated about what they do and do not like about each textbook," Hoffman says. "They use material developed from reading and discussing excerpts in support of their argument. To clearly argue for a particular author, students must understand the material." At the semester's end, each student is asked to write a two- to three-page proposal in which she recommends the "adoption" of one of the three textbooks she's surveyed. Her proposal must provide specific examples in support of the choice she makes.

In addition to giving students practice in reflective reading, these exercises help meet another, more "metacognitive" goal. As they're asked to critique the writing of published authors, students come to realize that the criteria they've established for assessing writing are truly universal. These criteria can be applied to the work of any author, no matter how skilled or practiced that author is. My students are always delighted to learn that even the best authors stand to gain from review and revision. This realization helps students to feel less reluctant about submitting their work for review by their peers.

I've noticed another benefit to exercises of this sort. In their first attempts at peer review, students are often hesitant to offer negative feedback, fearing that they will hurt the feelings of the author whose work they're reading. However, in the exercises we've just examined, the authors whose work is the subject of the students' review are not present in the room. This distance helps the students to be more forthcoming with critical comments. Eventually the students must learn to temper their criticisms to make them as respectful as they are helpful. However, the safety accorded them by the authors' absence helps them develop confidence to be more critical.

Structuring In-Class Peer Review

Once students have had a little practice in reviewing writing in an artificial setting, they will be ready to begin looking over one another's writing. It's best to ask students to do this peer review in class, at least at first. There are several benefits to doing this. First, you are present during the process, and you can help give the students direction as needed. Although you need not (and should not) intervene, you are on hand in case students have questions about the assignment or about review criteria. Second, students have the chance to see how others engage the review process. Every student in the class offers a model to every other, and each can learn from hearing the kinds of responses others give to their peers' work. Finally, in dedicating class time to peer review, you show your students that peer review is a worthwhile activity. After all, we have very little time to spend with our students in class over the course of the semester, and we must budget that time carefully. Therefore in giving even half of a class period to your students for the purpose of peer review, you send the message that this activity is important.

The mechanics of peer review are simple and permit numerous variations. In the simplest model, each student trades a draft of his work with one of his peers, and they take turns offering one another feedback on these drafts. For any piece of writing longer than a page or so, it may help to ask the students to read their partners' work before coming to class. Even if they make no comments on the draft during this initial reading, it will help to become familiar them with the writing they'll be critiquing.

The hard work then goes on in class. Since students may not have long to talk with one another, encourage them to focus on the major aspects of their peers' writing and not its specific details. One way to help students do this is to provide them with a summary of the criteria you and your students have agreed to use in assessing writing in your course. The most effective prompts will be questions requiring more than a yes/no answer:

- What appears to be the purpose of the writing? Identify two or three sentences that suggest that this is indeed the purpose.
- For what audience does your peer seems to be writing? What evidence supports this?
- Give an example of a place where the writing flows well. Give an example of a place where the writing flows poorly.
- Identify the strongest or most effective sentence in the writing. Identify the weakest or least effective sentence.

Nilson (2003) suggests a couple dozen similarly probing questions. She points out that these questions, by avoiding yes/no or good/bad dichotomies, do more than force deeper reading. They also enable students to respond to writing whose subject they may not even fully understand: an honest response to the each item requires only attention to the writing, not close familiarity with the writing's subject. Finally, they free students from having to make value judgments of one another's work, helping them to counter the anxiety they may feel about criticizing their peers' writing.

The sample list I include here will give you some idea of the aspects students might attend to in reading specific assignments. First, consider my department's senior seminar for mathematics majors. Students in this seminar review drafts of the expository paper each of them must complete by the semester's end. The primary criteria on the list I give these students conform closely to the "Four Cs" criteria discussed earlier in this chapter.

SENIOR SEMINAR PEER REVIEW CRITERIA

1. *Structure and composition.* Is the paper well composed?

   a. Does the paper have an introduction?

   b. Sketch a brief outline of your peer's paper as it's written. Does this outline provide a logical framework for your peer's project?

   c. What future directions does your peer indicate for her/his work?

   d. Are the transitions from paragraph to paragraph and from section to section smooth and logical ones? Give an example of a strong transition and an example of a weak transition.

2. *Purpose.* Is your peer's purpose for writing the paper made clear?

   a. Is there an abstract?

   b. Summarize your peer's main goal in one or two sentences.

   c. Does your peer explain the mathematical background surrounding the topic she/he is writing about? Indicate the areas of mathematics one would need to know and/or the courses one would need to have taken in order to understand the topic.

   d. Does your peer make clear how her/his work fits into that background? Summarize the contribution your peer is making in one or two sentences.

3. *Language and audience.*

   a. Is all notation and terminology defined and explained clearly? Give an example of a clear definition.

   b. Is notation and terminology used consistently?

   c. Does your peer's writing flow smoothly, and is it easy to understand? Give an example of a place where the writing flows smoothly. Give an example of a place where the writing does not flow smoothly.

   d. Does your peer avoid using "mathy" terms and jargon except when necessary? If appropriate, give a single example of a sentence or phrase that sounds "mathy."

   e. For what level of sophistication does your peer seem to be writing?

(continued)

4. *Correctness.* As you are not expected to be familiar with your peer's work (though I would like you to be able to understand your peer's paper), you may not be able to recognize outright mathematical errors. However, you should still be able to answer the following questions.

   a. Does your peer offer a proof (or a proof sketch) of all mathematical assertions she/he makes?

   b. If not, does she/he indicate where a proof might be found?

   c. Are there any obvious mathematical errors (adding and subtracting, counting, factoring, and so on) in your peer's work? Indicate two or three such errors, if you have found any.

The "subcriteria" given for each main criterion help students focus their reviews by giving them specific things to look for in their peers' writing. Such checklists are particularly helpful when students are reviewing projects with less familiar structure. In Chapter Five I mention such a project, in which students review one another's "grant proposals" with the help of a performance list.

Whatever kind of list you use, be sure that you provide your students with the list before they perform their peer reviews, ideally even before they begin writing. Having this list beforehand motivates students by letting them know precisely what is expected of their writing. With the review criteria in mind ahead of time, students will have a better understanding of the purpose of their writing, of their audience, and of the tone and style they should adopt.

Ongoing Peer Review: Homework Committees and Online Peer Review

Students can benefit from the opportunity to perform peer review in unsupervised settings as well. One means of offering this opportunity throughout the semester is through "homework committees," regular gatherings of students who meet to review their peers' drafts of yet-to-be-submitted homework sets. Another is through online peer review, mediated exchanges of homework or other assignments via email or course management software.

Homework Committees   Several faculty members in my department have adopted some version of this system during the past few years, and in every case, across a wide variety of courses at all levels, the adoption has proven successful. The basic structure of the system is simple and easy to implement. Moreover, it is applicable in any course in which students regularly submit some sort of written homework.

Out of every set of problems or proofs assigned, a number of them are designated as "committee problems." Students may submit drafts of solutions to these problems on a specified date several days before the homework is due. For each of these problems, three or four students will volunteer to serve on a committee that will meet to discuss all solutions to the given problem.

Each committee meets outside of class sometime before the next class meeting to discuss the solutions that have been submitted to them. During their meeting they offer written feedback to each solution's author. They check the solution against whatever criteria have been established for assessing writing and indicate the strengths and weaknesses of the solution. For my classes, I always make myself available for consultation should the committee need to discuss particularly tricky issues, but I always emphasize to my students that it is ultimately the committee's responsibility to verify each solution's quality.

After reviewing all of the solutions they've received, the committee writes a brief report on their overall impression of those solutions. I also ask them to provide me with a list of their peers whom they think made a substantial effort in completing a first draft of a solution. After returning their peers' drafts, the committee's last responsibility is to lead a brief in-class discussion on their problem. This discussion highlights the strengths and weaknesses of the solutions the committee received. I remind the students that it is not the committee's job to provide a correct solution during their discussion; this reminder encourages them to focus their attention on the process involved in creating the solutions they've read and not on the end product of that process.

Commented drafts in hand, the students now have until the next class meeting to perform revisions on these drafts, as needed. The students submit the revised committee problems, along with any problems not reviewed by committees, to me the next time we meet. From start to finish, a single cycle of homework committee activity might be structured as follows:

- First Monday: The homework set is first assigned.
- Wednesday: Students' submissions are due to the committee.

- Friday: The committee leads their in-class discussion.
- Second Monday: the entire homework set (including revised committee problems) is due.

To encourage students to participate in the process, I include their involvement in the committee process when I compute their class participation grades. For instance, I might ask each student to submit draft solutions to at least half of all committee problems and to serve on at least three homework committees during a given semester in order to receive full credit for participation.

Clearly homework committees help students develop the authority to assess the quality of one another's computations, explanations, and arguments, encouraging them to become more active agents in the generation of knowledge. Moreover, students learn a great deal about course concepts by serving on the committees. After all, each committee member will likely see several different methods of approaching whatever problem she's reviewing. Whether or not all of those methods are correct, each offers a different way of viewing the concepts the problem involves. As my students have pointed out, this benefit makes it worthwhile for a student to volunteer for those committees whose problems she doesn't fully understand. Finally, homework committees encourage students to get an earlier start on the homework; I've found students begin work on committee problems days before they would have begun their work had it not been subject to peer review.

Online Peer Review   Online exchanges of homework or other written assignments give students another opportunity to review one another's work and respond to it. If these exchanges take place in an open forum (like that provided by course management software such as Moodle, WebCT, or Blackboard), it is easy for you to observe and mediate the exchange as you wish, monitoring participation, giving credit to students who stand out as excellent reviewers, and offering encouragement to those who need it.

For each assignment subject to review, students post drafts of their work to a forum or to a discussion thread online. Each student is then given a set amount of time to review selected peers' work. You may assign students to one another's work in myriad ways: the assignment could be made randomly, for instance, or it could be made based upon the students' strengths and weaknesses as writers or as reviewers. You could instead pair students with peers whose writing style or structure differs dramatically from their own, challenging them to make sense of that different style.

While time may permit you to ask each student to read only a single peer's work, asking each student to review two or three of his classmates' writing has distinct advantages. First, if each student's writing is reviewed by two or three peers, that student will obtain multiple perspectives on his writing. It's unlikely every reviewer will respond to the same aspects of the writing, but multiple responses can help the student "triangulate" critical shortcomings. After all, though it's easy to dismiss one reviewer's comments as idiosyncratic or overly critical, when three reviewers raise similar concerns about a piece of writing, it is likely that revision to address those concerns is indicated.

Moreover, as with homework committees, when each student has an opportunity to review more than one of her peers' work, she will likely see very different ways of approaching a problem. This variety encourages students to think deeply about course concepts by reminding them that complicated problems rarely admit a single method of solution.

As noted previously, if the online exchange of drafts takes place in a forum you can monitor, it will be easy for you to track student participation. As with homework committees, this will enable you to require each student to play an active part in each review.

The next two chapters offer a wide variety of writing activities suitable for courses in nearly any quantitative discipline. In Chapter Four I focus on brief, informal writing-to-learn activities. If your goal isn't to craft a writing-intensive course but merely to introduce your students to some helpful reflective writing exercises, this chapter should give you many good ideas. In Chapter Five I introduce lengthier, more formal writing assignments. Though these assignments are more involved than those you'll find in Chapter Four, they have many of the elements of writing-to-learn. For all of these assignments, in both chapters, I provide hints on how to assess and respond to students' writing.

Low-Stakes Writing and Writing-to-Learn

In this chapter we encounter a wide variety of writing activities not typically found in quantitative courses. Many of these activities, however, have been well tested in more traditionally writing-intensive disciplines, and scholars of composition and rhetoric have spent many years in designing and refining them. The activities described here are often informal, and the writing that results from them may be loosely structured. They are often brief in duration and completed with little preparation on the part of the student or the teacher. Few of the activities we discuss in this chapter are meant to be graded carefully, if graded, or even read, at all. Rather, they are meant to be exercises in which students can freely explore ideas without fear of failure. For this reason this kind of writing is often called "low-stakes" writing: with little to lose by attempting to write, students can write more freely.

What benefits does low-stakes writing offer to the student? Freed from the fear of receiving low grades on their writing, students can use their writing in inventive and creative ways. They can use their writing to help them reflect on ideas discussed in class. They can use it to connect those ideas up with one another. They can use it to explore the consequences of course content more fully. In other words, they can use their writing to learn. It is this deep engagement with content that most easily justifies taking a few minutes of class time to complete a low-stakes exercise: students are not writing *instead of* learning about critical disciplinary ideas; they are writing *in order to* learn about those ideas.

Perhaps most important for those of us teaching in quantitative fields, low-stakes writing helps students overcome fear of writing. This kind of writing is brief and relatively painless, even to students who are reluctant to write. Low-stakes writing can even be fun. Indeed, several of the exercises I write about are playful and game-like (like texts, tweets, estimation essays, and fever-dream narratives). Many students in math-based disciplines come to those disciplines specifically because they enjoy playing with puzzles, and playful low-stakes writing activities can appeal strongly to these students.

What benefits does low-stakes writing offer to the instructor? This writing can be used to get a quick check on students' understanding. It can be used to identify the ideas students most easily grasp and those with which students are having the most difficulty. It can help propel a class discussion forward by allowing students to generate questions for discussion and to begin to formulate their own responses to those questions. Finally, as we've seen already, low-stakes writing can help students in the beginning stages of more formal writing projects. All of these benefits come to you without a great deal of time or effort on your part. For this reason low-stakes writing is the perfect place to start if you're not yet using writing in your courses but would like to bring it on board.

Indeed, many of the activities we explore in this chapter are suitable even for courses in which there otherwise is no substantial writing. Your course need not be designated as a writing-intensive course for your students to benefit from an occasional three-minute essay or freewrite. Moreover, it often adds little to your workload to ask your students to perform these exercises. Thus writing-to-learn activities can have a home in *any* disciplinary course.

I begin this chapter by describing a wide variety of low-stakes writing activities. I indicate ways each activity can fit into a quantitative course, providing specific examples for many activities. I then give some general comments on responding to low-stakes writing. Not all such writing requires a response from the instructor, and even when a response is called for, it need not be a lengthy one. Finally, I close the chapter with a brief list of readings and resources related to writing-to-learn; these resources will offer you many more ideas for using low-stakes writing in your classes. These and other works are included in the Recommended Readings and Resources section at the end of the book.

EXAMPLES OF LOW-STAKES WRITING ACTIVITIES

Let's take a look at some specific writing-to-learn activities. The list of activities I consider here is by no means an exhaustive one. If you're looking for more ideas, both John C. Bean's *Engaging Ideas: The Professor's Guide to Integrating Writing, Critical Thinking, and Active Learning in the Classroom* (1996) and Art Peterson's *The Writer's Workout Book: 113 Stretches Toward Better Prose* (1996) will give you many more examples of low-stakes writing exercises, many of which are easily adapted to quantitative classrooms. The resources sections at the end of this chapter and at the end of the book will give you access to many more examples.

Freewriting

Freewriting is a low-stakes writing technique developed by Peter Elbow (1973). Elbow pointed out that when we write we tend to ponder the words we use much more carefully than when we speak. Moreover, we take the time to compose those words into well-structured sentences, and those sentences into paragraphs, things we do not do when we speak. It's as though each of us has an "internal editor" who continually screens what we write as we write it.

Ordinary editors do more than rearrange words, though: they also offer authors advice on which ideas to include or exclude, and on which topics to focus. Our internal editors do these same things. As a result, according to Elbow, we often lose ideas we may have deleted before working them out more fully on paper. Though some of these ideas may have resulted in dead ends, others may have proven fruitful if given the chance to develop.

Freewriting's effectiveness stems from the way it helps us shut down our internal editors, allowing every idea that comes to mind to find its way onto the paper. There are a number of variations of freewriting, but the basic process is common to them all. First, choose a topic with which your freewrite will deal. Next, give yourself a fixed amount of time in which to write, five or ten minutes, for example. During that time, you are to write without stopping. Do not pause for any purpose, and write without regard for spelling, grammar, syntax, or choice of words. Write what comes to mind, and if at any point you're not sure of what to write next, simply write something like "I'm stuck I'm stuck I'm stuck" over and over until you become unstuck again. When your fixed time has elapsed, stop writing.

Coaching students in freewriting is fun, especially when they begin to realize its benefits. When first asked to freewrite, your students may find it difficult to shut down their internal editors. They may pause to find the right word, and they may cross out words they've written with which they're not satisfied. Your job as coach in these first few attempts is to help your students minimize their pauses. Encourage them to keep writing (a gentle nudge will usually do) and to keep everything they've written. Remind them that in this exercise, it's often the case that quantity is quality, since their goal should be to generate as many ideas as possible as they write.

The writing students produce during the freewriting process need not be shared with others, including you. This is the case particularly when students are asked to write on topics of a very personal nature. For example, on the first day of the semester I often ask my students to freewrite on their feelings about doing math. These feelings often include fear and frustration, and it may be difficult for students to own up to these feelings in front of a large group of strangers or to an unfamiliar instructor.

However, since freewriting helps the author discover ideas that otherwise may have gone unnoticed, it is sometimes helpful for students to share their freewritten ideas with one another. Thus you may consider asking your students to share not their writing itself but instead one or two of the insights or ideas they discovered through their writing: "Having finished your freewrite, select the three most intriguing ideas or phrases that came to you as you were writing. Share these ideas or phrases with the person sitting next to you." I give some specific examples of freewriting prompts later in the chapter.

Looping and Other Variations on Freewriting   *Looping* is a multistage version of freewriting. Begin the process as described. After your fixed writing time has elapsed, take a few minutes to look over the writing you've produced and identify one or two ideas that stand out in some way. Does something you've written surprise you? Shock you? Amuse you? Make a note of these ideas, and choose one that is particularly outstanding. Copy this idea down below the writing you've just completed. Now begin writing again, for another fixed length of time, using the topic you have just selected as the prompt for a new freewrite.

You may repeat this process as many times as you would like to, continuing to uncover new ideas and develop them more fully. When my students are freewriting as a brainstorming exercise, I often ask them to complete three iterations. After the last period of freewriting, I ask them to reflect on all of the writing they've done and gather from it any observations they find helpful to them. I then prompt them to team up with one or two of their classmates and share these observations.

Todd Findley introduced a freewriting-like writing exercise he called the "fever dream" (2011). The process he describes is meant to help students craft a personal autobiography, but you can easily adapt it to address other topics. Findley asks students to begin by laying out a visual timeline of their lives and then puts them in the mood to write by playing some music or poetry that "shows how the psychic innards of a writer's life can be biopsied and made into art . . . to be read as a *single driving sentence,* an approach that makes a fine transition to the next step" (emphasis his). Findley then asks each student to select one event from her timeline on which she will write one page, as quickly as possible. Her writing will be bound by one rule only: the entire page must comprise a *single* sentence. This rule is designed to have the same effect as freewriting, encouraging the writer to ignore grammatical conventions as she pushes forward with her ideas. The writing that results will likely have a frenetic, passionate feel to it, as though the writer is hallucinating from the effects of a raging fever.

Yet another variation on freewriting, particularly useful in the quantitative disciplines, allows the writer to use more than words in her composition. I have found it helpful to encourage my students to include visual elements of various kinds (graphs, diagrams, and so forth) in their freewrites. For example, in my mathematics courses, when I ask students to freewrite to generate potential solutions to a problem I have posed to them, I encourage them to draw graphs, jot down formulas, and record any other information that comes to mind as they write uninterruptedly. This sort of activity calls on what Dunn (2001) would call "multiple literacies," as students learn how to inform their written composition with ideas gained through reasoning visually and spatially as well as verbally.

Uses for Freewriting in Quantitative Disciplines Freewriting is a powerful writing-to-learn technique. There are a number of ways you can use it in the quantitative classroom, and I offer only a few examples of these uses. For further examples, see Olds, Dyrud, Held, and Sharp (1993) and Ostheimer, Mylrea, and Lonsdale (1994), both addressing freewriting in engineering; Bossavit and Gaillot (2005) and Deremer (1993), both addressing freewriting in computer science; and King (1982), addressing freewriting in mathematics. I am sure you will be able to come up with many more examples of your own.

Writing a discipline-specific "autobiography." Ask your students to freewrite about their experience in the discipline your course deals with. Let them write not only about the courses they have taken and the topics they have studied but also about how they felt about their study in those courses and topics. This exercise is a great first-day activity, especially for students who are anxious about math-based courses. The exercise allows your students an easy entry into your course and can be used to let students get to know each other better if asked to share their freewritten work.

Connecting the old with the new. Freewriting gives students an excellent opportunity to brainstorm ways that familiar techniques can be applied in unfamiliar settings. Freewriting can also provide an excellent segue from one topic to another: ask your students to focus their freewrite on ways to connect the old topic to the new one. For example, in an abstract algebra course, I might ask students to freewrite on the concept of a "ring" shortly after this concept is introduced, focusing on the way in which rings relate to the by-then-familiar concept of a "group." Although this exercise is unlikely to result in any rigorous proofs, it helps students gain familiarity with the new idea by comparing it to one that's come before.

Developing an intuitive description of a technical fact or theorem. Students understand technical ideas more fully when they are asked to put them into their own words. Freewrites offer students the perfect place to begin that paraphrasing process. Students can be asked to freewrite about why lasers work, about what they might infer from a particular set of statistical data, or about why the Mean Value Theorem ultimately makes sense. Five minutes spent in freewriting on these or any other abstract concept will help students form more concrete versions of the concept in their minds.

As a lead-in to a more substantial writing assignment. I introduced freewriting in Chapter Two as one of several prewriting strategies. Freewriting can help students come up with topics for further writing without dismissing them out of hand. For example, at the outset of each "chapter" of the student-authored textbook assignment I describe in Chapter Five, I give students a chance to freewrite on potential topics for inclusion before engaging in a full-class brainstorming discussion.

Doubting and Believing

Another of Peter Elbow's many contributions to writing-to-learn is the "doubting and believing game" (1986), an exercise students can perform in or outside of the classroom. This writing activity can help students form a critical response to a reading, lecture, or discussion. Doubting and believing is designed to allow students to overcome trained skepticism by asking them to respond to a reading in two different ways, first as a "believer," then as a "doubter."

We spend much of our time training our students to be skeptical and critical and to find flaws in arguments placed before them. Therefore as "believers" of a reading, students take on an academically uncharacteristic role. In this role students are asked to accept uncritically the propositions the author of their reading puts before them. While reading, students write an explanation of the author's thesis and arguments, summarizing these in their own words. Although it may seem irresponsible at first, "belief" can go a long way in the quantitative disciplines. Rather than focusing on the minutiae of proof or verification, students can focus on what might lie beyond the author's thesis, on its "big picture" implications and consequences. Students develop a great deal of intuition in this way.

Having finished their role as "believers," the students next become "doubters," responding to their reading by questioning everything and taking nothing for granted. Now they should be on the lookout for holes in the author's argument, gaps in her logic, or other problems. Reading in this "doubting" way can lead students to a deeper technical understanding of the work they are responding to. Students should summarize all of their criticisms of the reading, placing their doubting summary alongside the believing summary they've crafted just before.

Finally, the students reflect on both of their summaries and come to their own conclusion, writing their own take on the reading. Having examined the reading from two thoroughly different points of view, the students should be well equipped to recognize both the strengths and the weaknesses of the reading. This final exercise helps students find their own voice as they write, and the resulting writing will therefore be authentic.

As a variation, you might instead ask the students to "stay in character" and write two brief responses to the reading, one as a believer and one as a doubter. This exercise can help students to see that two seemingly contrary points of view may both have validity in some way. It also helps them to recognize the way in which the purpose of a piece of writing affects the way in which that piece is written. Indeed, they're sure to find that their "believing" responses differ from their "doubting" responses in tone and language.

Uses for Doubting and Believing in Quantitative Disciplines   The following examples demonstrate some of the ways doubting and believing can help students approach course content.

For a calculus course.   "Read our textbook's discussion of the Mean Value Theorem, first as a believer and then as a doubter. Use your believing and doubting summaries as a basis for writing a half-page discussion of the theorem."

For a mathematical finance course.   "To prepare for our next class, select one of the pricing models we have discussed during the past week. Write two responses to this model, one as a believer and one as a doubter. In your believing response, highlight at least two consequences you can derive by assuming your model's truth. In your doubting response, attack your model by pointing out at least two weak points in the model. We will use your responses as a basis for discussion in class."

For a course in algorithm design.   "Read our textbook's discussion of Dijkstra's algorithm for finding a minimal spanning tree of a graph, first as a believer and then as a doubter. Take notes as you read. Once done, write a one-page 'believing' response in which you accept the truth of the algorithm and describe at least two potential applications of the algorithm that are not discussed by the text. Finally, write a one-page 'doubting' response in which you confront each point of the author's argument that seems questionable to you. Explain each questionable point in your own words and provide an illustrative example to help your reader understand the point."

Microgenres: Three-Minute Themes, Texts, and Tweets

A *three-minute theme* is a very brief piece of focused writing that can serve any number of purposes in the classroom. Give your students a specific prompt for their writing, and give them a short amount of time, no more than a few minutes, to respond to the prompt. Because the students have very little time to write, you may wish to give them specific direction regarding the form of writing you expect from them:

- "Write three sentences. In the first, indicate one or two topics from the previous reading that you find most confusing. In the second, indicate the topic you feel most confident about. In the final sentence, indicate a potential application of the topic you mentioned in your second sentence."

- "Write two sentences. In the first, indicate the example from today's class that made the most sense to you. In the second sentence, indicate the example that made the least sense."

- "Your best friend is sick in bed and was unable to come to class today. She's asked you to let her know what went on as soon as you can. Write a text message to her summarizing today's discussion. Your message can contain no more than 160 characters."

As these examples demonstrate, three-minute themes provide an excellent means of reflecting on readings or discussions and of checking students' understanding of those readings or discussions. The themes take little more time for you to read than it took the students to write them, and in a few minutes' time you can get a clear picture of the difficulties students are facing.

The last example suggests a variation on this activity that can take place outside of class, when students have more time to write. Text messages, Facebook status updates (on www.facebook.com), tweets (posts on the social networking website Twitter, www.twitter.com), and other electronic genres have become so familiar as "short forms" or "microgenres" that we need not shy away from asking our students to write in these forms. The extreme brevity of these media forces the writer to pay very careful attention to his choice of words. This brevity also encourages creative combinations of words and symbols as the writer tries to convey rich ideas in as little space as possible.

Students also find these genres fun, for they open up a space in which students can use language more creatively and playfully. As a particularly playful example, my colleague Jean Marie Linhart of Texas A&M University shares this 113-character tweet, written in "leetspeak" by linear algebra student Andrew Bohuslav: "4 b4515 15 7|-|3 5/\/\4LL357 L1|\|34R 1|\|D3P3|\|D3|\|T 5P4|\|\|1|\|9 537 0PH 4 \/3(70R 5P4(3)r PhR33 /\/\0DUL3." (Translation: "A basis is the smallest linear independent spanning set of a vector space or free module.")

Uses for Three-Minute Themes and Other Microgenres in Quantitative Disciplines   It's not hard to find ways to work such simple exercises into other quantitative courses, as the following examples demonstrate.

- *For a physics course.* "Suppose that you are 'liveblogging' your reading of the chapter of our textbook dealing with electromagnetism. For each section in the chapter write a tweet summarizing the most important idea of that section. Remember that a tweet can be no more than 140 characters in length."

- *For a thermodynamics course.* "Summarize both Clausius's and Kelvin's statements of the Second Law of Thermodynamics in 160 characters or less, so that your summary can be sent as a text message."

- *For a statistics course.* "Write a Facebook status update reminding your friends about the study session you are organizing for your peers. The update should list the most important topics from the chapter on variance in no more than 420 characters."

As these examples show, writing in such circumscribed form forces students to zero in on the most important points in a reading or discussion. This focus can help them construct outlines for more substantial writing projects or make the most out of their study time. Furthermore, these simple exercises, in which students write for a specific "reader," help students to become more aware of how the form of their writing is determined by the audience for whom they write.

Bean (1996) gives many more examples of microthemes' use, and you can find many more ways to integrate digital media into your classroom in Beach, Anson, Kastman-Breuch, and Swiss (2009) and Parker (2010). Both of these books describe ways to help our students' familiarity with new and emerging media turn these media into powerful teaching tools. The latter book is aimed at middle school and high school teachers, but many of the exercises it contains can be adapted to college classrooms with little difficulty.

Dialogues

A great deal of the scholarly writing we craft, including textbooks and academic articles, is inherently unidirectional. Though the scholarly writer may use various rhetorical devices to try to bring the reader into the conversation, the discourse remains one-sided. No matter how many times the writer asserts that "we" see the result of a physical experiment or "we" complete the final steps of a mathematical proof, the writer is always the agent, and the readers are merely observers. This one-sided mode of communication has an aura of expertise and professionalism. Students can be put off by this tone, and they can feel robbed of their creative agency and incapable of playing an active part in disciplinary discovery. This exclusion can leave them feeling "voiceless," as though they have nothing to contribute to the conversations going on in your class.

You can help students find their voices, literally, by asking them to write short dialogues in which the speakers discuss course concepts using everyday conversational language. This sort of language can help students gain intuitive understanding of technical ideas, making a dialogue an excellent analytic exercise. A dialogue requires two voices, over both of which the student has control. Neither of these needs to be the speaker's real voice, for ultimately the dialogue is a sort of play-acting or fiction. This fiction offers students a measure of safety. For instance, the student can safely use one speaker's voice to express her own uncertainty and confusion. This speaker can ask the simple questions with obvious answers the student herself likely has; this speaker can trip over obvious obstacles or pose potential problems. In this way the student can unashamedly admit to having difficulties with course concepts. With the other voice in her dialogue, the student can adopt an authoritative role. The student's other speaker helps her conversation partner toward a better understanding during the course of their talk together.

Students are not accustomed to writing in two distinct voices, and they will need practice and coaching to help them craft effective dialogues. I have found that without encouragement students will often fall back into writing in a more traditional one-sided manner. One speaker in the conversation will say little more than "I see" and "Oh, I get it!" while the other speaker lectures away. I have also found that students need to be reminded not to simply parrot the language of their textbooks. As one purpose of a dialogue is to help students develop intuitive (and not technical) understanding, they gain little from the exercise if they resort to excerpting their texts.

Uses for Dialogues in Quantitative Disciplines   Here are some sample prompts for dialogues in a variety of quantitative courses. Brown (1986) gives more examples as he details his success at using dialogues in a course introducing students to mathematical proof.

For a linear algebra course.   "Your best friend (who is also enrolled in our Linear Algebra) is having trouble interpreting determinants geometrically. 'I get the numbers,' he says, 'but I just don't see what they mean.' Write a dialogue in which you help him understand the geometric meaning of the determinant of a 3×3 matrix."

For an advanced economics course.   "While reviewing for our upcoming exam, you and a friend begin debating the Lucas critique of macroeconomics. 'Lucas was right,' you say. 'There's no way we can make these broad sweeping claims based on all of these individual little data.' 'I don't know what you're talking about,' your friend says. 'I think Lucas was full of it.' Write a dialogue in which you attempt to convince your friend that Lucas's critique is a valid one. Your dialogue should include specific examples to help you make your point, but it may also raise potential objections to Lucas's critique."

For a first-semester physics course. "Your best friend has asked you for help with her physics homework. 'I'm not sure I see what Newton's Laws of Motion mean. I just can't get a grip on them.' Write a dialogue in which you help your friend understand each of Newton's laws. Your dialogue should include an intuitive example for each law."

For a statistics course. "Your friend is distraught. It's the night before your statistics exam, and he still doesn't understand the difference between stratified sampling and cluster sampling. 'I don't see why you need to use one or the other at all,' he tells you. 'Why don't you just pick your population completely at random?' Write a dialogue in which you help your friend to see the differences between these methods of sampling, illustrating the differences with specific examples where appropriate."

For a physical chemistry course. "You and your best friend are preparing for an upcoming chemistry quiz on the structure of the atom. 'I know she's going to ask about the Rutherford model and the Bohr model,' your friend insists. 'I honestly don't know what the difference is. I mean, isn't the Rutherford model good enough? Why did Bohr even bother?' Write a dialogue in which you help your friend understand the differences between the two models."

Estimation Essays: Quantitative Analysis Through Writing

Given the ubiquity of calculators and powerful, relatively easy-to-use scientific software, our students are often unaccustomed to manipulating quantitative data without the help of technology. Nevertheless, being able to deal with these data fluently, at least as approximations, is an invaluable skill for them to develop. Being able to ignore the numerical data altogether, in order to focus on the underlying processes in which those data are used, is a yet more important skill.

"Estimation essays" ask students to track quantitative data from one stage of a complex process to the next. In writing estimation essays, students do not perform precise computations. Instead they describe how to deal with rounded figures and orders of magnitude. They also learn how to deal with uncertainties and absent data. In writing their essays, students may find they have been given only some of the information needed to develop a fully accurate solution, and their essays must then describe how to obtain an optimal answer in the absence of that data. Perhaps most important, estimation essays help students develop problem-solving skills: since students are no longer focused on precise numerical values, their attentions shift to developing the processes into which those values, if known, would be plugged.

An assignment I give students on the first day of my second-semester calculus course gives an example of this sort of exercise. Before the first day of class I place a small coin-operated gumball machine (the sort with a glass globe) full of small candies in the department's math assistance center. Here students will have access to the machine for several hours each day. By the end of the first week of the semester, each student must write an essay in which she describes how to obtain an estimate for the number of candies in the machine's glass globe. The value the student obtains is relatively unimportant; what's important is that the student clearly articulates her process.

Coming up with a valid process is no easy task. Though students are free to take whatever measurements they would like to, both of the machine and of the candies inside, several factors complicate their measurements. The glass globe is irregularly shaped, as are the candies (I never choose candies that are simple spheres). Moreover, there is some variation in the size of the candies, and there is a considerable amount of airspace between the individual candies in the globe. These complications force students to deal with approximations rather than exact figures. They force the students to focus on the process of their solutions rather than on specific numerical values.

Though there is no single correct method to solve this problem, the most accurate estimates students provide are usually obtained through some kind of Riemann sum, a concept at the heart of integral calculus. Thus, in addition to getting the students to think creatively about mathematical processes, the project reinforces ideas critical to the course.

Uses for Estimation Essays in Quantitative Disciplines   Here are some sample prompts for estimation essays in other disciplines.

For a genomics course. "Recall that a *bit* is the amount of information conveyed in a simple 'yes/no' response, and that a *byte* is a unit equivalent to 8 bits. (For example, it takes 5 bits to communicate a single letter of the English alphabet unambiguously.) Using what we've learned about the chemical and mathematical structure of human chromosomes, come up with an estimate for the amount of information (in bits) conveyed by the third chromosome. You certainly don't have enough information to obtain a precise figure, but feel free to make any assumptions you need as you derive your estimate, defending those assumptions as you make them."

For a course in database design. "You have been hired to design a database to track personnel data for a company with approximately 2,000 employees. Ten fields are to be maintained for each employee. Derive an estimate for the space you would need to store the necessary data in a heap, explaining each step of the process you use to derive your estimate. Then repeat the exercise, assuming you would store the data in a clustered index instead."

For a number theory course. "We now know that the Prime Number Theorem gives an asymptotic estimate for the number of prime numbers less than or equal to a given integer *x*. Recall that a *twin prime pair* is a pair of prime numbers that differ by 2 from one another. (For example, 3 and 5 are a twin prime pair, as are 5 and 7.) Generate a list of all of the twin prime pairs both of whose values are less than each of the following values: 100, 1000, 10000, and 100000. Use your list and the Prime Number Theorem to come up with a reasonable asymptotic estimate for the number of twin prime pairs less than or equal to a given number *x*. Explain your reasoning carefully; this reasoning and your explanation of it are more important than obtaining the correct answer."

Journaling

Journal writing gives students a chance to craft an ongoing account of their growth as practitioners of a particular discipline. By journaling regularly on course content and their engagement with it, students create a reflective space in which they can achieve numerous learning outcomes:

- Explore, interrogate, synthesize, and analyze the concepts central to the course
- Develop an intuitive understanding of technical definitions, theories, and formulas

- Provide the instructor with feedback on their understanding of course content
- Reflect affectively on their engagement with course content, rather than cognitively

This last effect is a critical one that is often overlooked. A number of studies (see, for example, Hackett & Betz, 1989; Hannula, Maijala, & Pehkonen, 2004; and Hembree, 1990) have uncovered a strong correlation between student confidence and student performance in science coursework. Simply put, the more confidently a student pursues her studies, the more competently she'll perform, and the more likely she'll be to see herself as an agent, capable of creating ideas rather than simply receiving them. Giving students an opportunity to reflect not only on what they've learned but also on how they're learning it and how they feel about their understanding can help them build confidence in themselves as learners.

The journal genre permits tremendous variation, and no two instructors will assign exactly the same journaling activity to their students. Students' journals can be maintained and submitted electronically or in handwritten form. (Though the former may be more convenient and less messy, the latter permits students to include visual elements and specialized notation more easily.) Students may be asked to respond to daily prompts, weekly prompts, or more infrequent prompts still.

Most important, the flexibility of the genre makes journals an excellent tool for working toward a broad variety of learning goals. Here are some specific sample applications.

- Students can use journals to respond to assigned readings and identify the most important aspects of those readings. *Sample prompt:* "On Monday in class we will discuss a method for computing the eigenvalues and eigenvectors of a given matrix. To prepare for this class, read the section of our textbook that focuses on this method. In your journal, indicate what you believe are the most important aspects of that process."
- Students can use journals to tie together ideas from recent classes and organize ideas for upcoming classes. *Sample prompt:* "Today in class we discussed a method for computing the eigenvalues and eigenvectors of a given matrix. On Wednesday we will practice applying this method. To prepare for Wednesday's class, outline in your journals the steps of method we discussed. Explain briefly, in your own words, why each step follows logically from the last."

- The instructor can use students' journal responses to identify students' strengths and weaknesses. This can help the instructor focus attention on the concepts students are having the most trouble with. *Sample prompt:* "Today in class we practiced applying the method for computing the eigenvalues and eigenvectors of a given matrix. Identify the single step of this process you feel most confident about and describe it briefly in your journal. Also, identify the single step of this method you are most confused about and explain briefly what about it you find confusing."

Despite the obvious benefits they offer to students, many instructors worry that the extra time responding to journals may make their assignment untenable. However, not every journal entry must be responded to, or even read. Indeed, if you grade journals at all, you may not wish to grade them for content, but only for completion. This policy keeps the stakes low and ensures that students will feel freer to respond openly and honestly to the prompts you give them. Alternatively, students should expect that any given journal entry they write may be read and responded to, but that a week or two may pass without one of their entries being selected for response. Moreover, students should understand that you expect their entries to be substantive ones and not simply peremptory responses to the prompts you give for guidance. In return, when you respond to your students' journal entries, you respond not as an assessor but as a mentor, with an eye toward helping your students grow as practitioners of your discipline. You respond not to grade but rather to guide. I find that it takes no more than an hour a week to read and respond to a substantial number of students' journal entries.

The literature on the use of journals in quantitative disciplines is quite robust. Anson and Beach (1995) treat journals in an arbitrary classroom setting, but many of the principles and practices they discuss are applicable to quantitative courses. Gardner and Fulwiler (1998) address teachers in technical areas and offer accounts of journal use in several quantitative fields, including engineering and computer science. Many of the articles included in this volume give specific examples of prompts and helpful suggestions for responding to students' journal entries. Yet further ideas for journals can be found in Audet, Hickman, and Dobrynina (1996, in physics); Brewer and Jozefowicz (2007, in economics); Sgoutas-Emch and Johnson (1998, in statistics); and Sharp, Harb, and Terry (1997, in engineering).

Daybooks

Like a journal, a daybook is an episodic record of a writer's thoughts. However, the structure of a daybook is remarkably more fluid than that of a journal. In a journal, the writer responds to specific prompts or requests for feedback. In a daybook, the writer writes whenever he feels an urge to do so, and this writing takes no definite shape. As Brannon and her coauthors put it, "We think of the daybook like that drawer in the kitchen where we stick everything that does not yet have a place, but we know we might need someday. . . . The daybook serves as the place where the students put all of their thoughts throughout the day" (2008, p. 11). Daybooks offer the writer a place for ongoing reflection, a place where numerous thoughts are collected in one place and allowed to simmer together in a sort of creative stew.

I have colleagues who carry a daybook (in the form of a notebook or composition book) with them wherever they go, to class, to meetings, and to conferences and workshops. As they are almost never without the daybook, it becomes the perfect place to jot down anything that comes to mind, when it comes to mind. Meeting minutes, notes, and ideas for future research or class discussions all find their way into a daybook's pages. My colleague Kerri Flinchbaugh even carries a glue stick so that she can paste in outside objects (handouts, clippings from articles or other sources, photos, and so on), helping her to create a rich multimedia narrative. To use a musical metaphor, if a text-only journal is a sonata, then a daybook is a symphony.

For students in quantitative courses, daybooks can serve as messy records of their random thoughts, insights, observations, and recollections as they go about the business of learning. The multimedia potential of daybooks makes them the perfect place for students to reflect both in words and in pictures about concepts that come up in their coursework. Students can include class notes, supplemented by doodles, data, diagrams, graphs, and charts. They can include the scratchwork they do in trying to solve a homework problem from calculus, or the computations they perform as they convert their observations from a chemistry experiment into a narrative describing that experiment's results. They can include the random ruminations that come to them as they eat breakfast before their eight o'clock economics class, or a schematic of the electric circuit design that came to them at midnight on the night before.

It is unlikely that students will use their daybooks in this fashion without considerable prompting and preparation. To help them realize daybooks' potential usefulness, you may do well at first to assign specific tasks requiring their use. The following examples can get you started; Brannon et al. (2008) contains many more ideas. Although that book is aimed primarily at K–12 teachers, much of what is said there is equally applicable in college classrooms.

- Ask your students to do the scratchwork for a particular homework set in their daybooks and then to submit the daybooks when submitting the homework set. This will help them to see that you value the process needed to obtain a correct answer as highly as you value the answer itself.

- Whenever students perform freewrites or other low-stakes writing you won't need to read, ask them to do so in their daybooks rather than on whatever random scrap of paper they have on hand. Doing this will ensure they'll have a record of their freewritten thoughts to which they can later return as needed. This will be particularly helpful if this writing is done in preparation for more involved projects later on.

- Ask students to find examples of real-world instances of course concepts and paste them into their daybooks: newspaper articles illustrating economic principles or inferential statistics, photographs suggesting violation of physical laws, photographs of buildings whose construction requires civil engineering considerations discussed in class. These examples can then be used to drive class discussions.

You can respond to students' daybooks much as you would respond to their journals, always valuing process over product. It's not so important *what* the students choose to include in their daybooks as *that* they choose to include something when appropriate. Once students realize the freedom a daybook affords, and once they realize how handily it serves as a single-place repository for the ideas they come up with in your course, they will compose in them more and more frequently without your requiring them to do so.

Time Capsule Letters

By the end of one of your courses, your students will have grown as practitioners of your discipline. Ideally, they also will have grown as learners. To get the most out of your course, your students will have adjusted the way they study, the way they read and write, and the way they think. They will have left behind whatever habits they didn't find helpful, and they will have developed new ones as they learned how best to learn in your course. By the course's end these students have become the experts on learning in that course. Why not let them pass their new-found wisdom on to future "generations" of learners? "Time capsule letters" give your students a chance to do just that.

At the end of the semester, ask your students to write one last piece, a letter addressed to the students who will enroll in your course the next time it's offered. In these letters, your students give advice on how to succeed in your course, as though the letters will be placed in a time capsule to be opened by future students. Early in the term the next time you teach the same course, ask your students to read the letters left to them by the previous class. You may even ask the new students to write on the letters they've read, reflecting on the advice that makes most sense to them.

The new students are likely to take these letters seriously. After all, your former students have greater credibility than you do when it comes to dispensing advice. It's one thing for you to give your students tips on dealing with the difficult concepts in your course; it's another thing for former students, your current students' peers, to do the same. Moreover, since no two students learn in the same way, new students reading the collection of letters left to them will see a wide array of study techniques. They will also notice themes that arise over and over in many different letters. Students will be wise to note those themes.

The letter-writing exercise has benefits for the students writing the letters, too. Reflecting on the way they've learned in your course helps students to recognize the study habits that are most helpful to them, reinforcing those habits. They can take these habits with them to their future courses.

I have assigned this exercise in several classes, and I am always impressed by the quality of the advice students give to their peers. While much of the advice is standard and predictable (along the lines of "Keep up the homework," "Ask for help in the math lab," and so forth), some of it is strikingly deep. For example, one past student's account of the way she approached a new mathematical proof read like a textbook description of the writing process, including prewriting, review, and revision. Of course, she didn't use technical terms like these, and her language was straightforward and easy to read. The down-to-earth advice she gave her peers was far more authentic than, and just as helpful as, any I could ever offer.

I have also given a mid-semester version of the exercise in which students give advice, anonymously, to their peers in the current class. This exercise helps the stronger students offer pointers to the weaker students while there's still time to adjust the way they do their work. Even students who are not doing particularly well in the course are often aware of how their performance could be made better, and the exercise helps them reflect on ways to improve their study habits before the semester ends.

NOTES ON RESPONDING TO LOW-STAKES WRITING

Since so much low-stakes writing is done simply to help students learn, often there is little reason for you to respond to it at all, and there is certainly little reason for you to grade it. Some exercises (such as freewriting) are simply meant to help the student generate ideas and organize them. Other exercises (such as three-minute themes, doubt and believing, and time capsule letters) are meant to help you check students' understanding of basic course concepts and to help the students check their own understanding. None of these exercises requires a response from you, although you may give a brief response if you feel it necessary to correct students' misunderstandings or to provide additional guidance. Alternatively, you may group all students' responses into rough categories and give a brief response to each category: "Students in this group may wish to review the definition of X. . . . Students in this group showed that they understand X, but don't see how it connects to Y. . . ." These responses can be given on a course website or verbally at the next meeting of the class.

Moreover, sometimes there is no need for you to even *read* the work your students produce in completing writing-to-learn activities. This work is often very disorganized and difficult to read. It can sometimes be very personal, and sometimes so idiosyncratic that it makes sense only to the writer herself. If you choose to read your students' work, make sure you let them know this in advance. When they know their work will be read by another they will take more care to ensure that it's legible and not so personal that they will be reluctant to share it with you.

Even if you do respond to your students' writing, your responses can be simple ones, depending on the purpose the writing serves. If the writing is meant to check students' understanding, your responses can give direction to students who seem to be veering off course, and they can give positive reinforcement to students who make good progress. If the writing is meant to help students generate ideas, your responses can encourage them to reflect on, organize, and build upon the ideas they've already come up with. All of this can often be done in a word or two, with a well-placed "What?" "Why?" and "Yes!"

It may be appropriate to give credit to students for completing some of the more time-consuming or labor-intensive forms of low-stakes writing. It is appropriate to give credit for any sort of writing with more than momentary importance, and for any sort of writing that serves one or more course learning goals. For instance, suppose you ask your students to write in a journal regularly. They may produce dozens of pages of reflective writing over the course of the semester, and this writing has not only helped the students to learn; it has also helped them demonstrate to you their mastery of course concepts. Giving students credit for completing this work, even if it's little more than an "X" or a checkmark on every third journal entry, shows that you value that work highly enough to keep track of whether or not students complete it. Keep in mind that students should feel safe using low-stakes writing activities to explore ideas freely and without consequence. Therefore if you grade such writing at all, your grades should be based exclusively on the students' completion of the writing and not on its correctness.

Many of the writing activities addressed here can easily be submitted online. Not only does this form of submission make it easy for you to respond to students' work; it also allows students to read each others' work, when appropriate, and to generate discussions about the ideas they write about. These discussions can serve as the engines of further invention and discovery as students engage in the social construction of disciplinary knowledge.

The low-stakes writing activities we've considered here are only a handful of the hundreds developed by instructors in disciplines across the college curriculum. You can consult any of the suggested readings at the end of this chapter and at the end of the book if you're interested in reading about more writing-to-learn activities. Furthermore, I have no doubt you will also be able to come up with a few low-stakes activities of your own. With a little trial and error, and a bit of tweaking when appropriate, you should have no trouble designing the writing-to-learn exercises that most effectively aid the novice writers in your discipline.

Depending on your goals for writing in your course, you may see no need to go beyond the activities introduced in this chapter. Indeed, if your aim is not to make your course into a writing-intensive one, but merely to give students simple opportunities to use writing as a learning tool, this chapter may given you all the help you need. However, writing, even writing-to-learn, can take on much more elaborate forms, as you will find in the following chapter, where we examine more formal writing activities for quantitative courses.

READINGS AND RESOURCES

The following sources are general ones, treating a wide variety of writing-to-learn exercises; sources on specific types of exercises were given throughout the chapter. Some of the following sources (Countryman, 1992, and Peterson, 1996, for instance) are aimed at instructors of writing at the middle or high school level. However, many of the exercises these sources describe are applicable in college courses too.

Bean, J. C. *Engaging Ideas: The Professor's Guide to Integrating Writing, Critical Thinking, and Active Learning in the Classroom.* San Francisco: Jossey-Bass, 1996.

Belanoff, P., Elbow, P., and Fontaine, S. L. (eds). *Nothing Begins with N: New Investigations of Freewriting.* Carbondale: Southern Illinois University Press, 1991.

Cooney, T. J., and Hirsch, C. R. (eds). *Writing to Learn Mathematics and Science.* New York: Teachers College Press, 1989.

Countryman, J. *Writing to Learn Mathematics: Strategies That Work, K–12.* Portsmouth, NH: Heinemann, 1992.

Elbow, P. *Writing Without Teachers.* New York: Oxford University Press, 1973.

Gottschalk, K., and Hjortshoj, K. T*he Elements of Teaching Writing: A Resource for Instructors in All Disciplines.* Boston: Bedford/St. Martin's, 2004.

Leist, S. M. *Writing to Teach; Writing to Learn in Higher Education.* Lanham, MD: University Press of America, 2006.

Peterson, A. *The Writer's Workout Book: 113 Stretches Toward Better Prose.* Berkeley, CA: Nation Writing Project, 1996.

WAC Clearinghouse, http://wac.colostate.edu.

Formal Writing Projects

While the previous chapter dealt with brief, low-stakes writing exercises, the present chapter concerns more carefully structured, and generally lengthier, projects. There are often close ties between the two: as I mentioned in the previous chapter, informal writing (in the form of freewriting, journaling, and so forth) can often prove useful in the prewriting stages of more involved writing projects. Moreover, some writing projects, like the "Great Debates" project introduced in this chapter, involve components of varying levels of formality and elaboration.

The writing projects addressed here are suitable for use in a wide variety of courses in quantitative fields. I focus on projects that do not conform to more "traditional" genres (like expository papers or research articles). Those genres are treated more fully elsewhere, and they are familiar enough to most of us that little introduction to them is necessary. My goal here is to offer some fresh ideas for projects to challenge your students to use writing in creative ways that will stimulate their thinking about your discipline. In completing these, your students will use writing as a means of learning and not simply as a means of communicating ideas. It is for this reason that these writing assignments have value in our courses: the time students spend in completing these assignments is not taken away from the time they spend learning course content. Rather, these assignments enhance student learning by serving as a lens through which course content is viewed.

For each of the following projects I give some tips for structuring the project effectively and for responding to your students' work on the project. I also indicate some of the learning goals the project helps to meet. For some projects I've given hints as to how those projects may be adapted to courses in specific disciplines. Though not every project will be suitable for every course, I am certain you will find some that are useful for your own classes.

WRITING ON WRITING

Writing about writing can be a very valuable exercise. (See, for example, Downs & Wardle, 2007, where a very convincing argument is made for this claim.) This is particularly true in quantitative disciplines, which are famous, even infamous, for their reliance on lofty language. The language we use is a necessarily rich one, full of technical terms. The words we use when we communicate our ideas to one another have unambiguous meanings that are often hard to master. Words whose everyday meanings are fluid and flexible, like *ball*, *bond*, or *neighborhood*, are used with precision by the mathematician, the chemist, or the physicist. Students unaccustomed to the exactness of technical terms like these experience difficulty in reading and writing in our disciplines simply because they are not yet familiar with the precise meanings of the words they encounter.

Beginning writers in any discipline can benefit from "metacognitive" exercises that invite them to reflect on the meanings of the words they read and write frequently. Close examination of disciplinary discourse not only helps students gain mastery of technical terminology; it also makes them more aware of the everyday meanings of the words they use in other disciplines and encourages them to pay attention to their choice of words in any kind of writing.

I have given students a variety of assignments in which they are asked to reflect on the precise meanings of the words they use in conveying mathematical ideas. The "Good Writing/Bad Writing" exercise I described in Chapter Three is one such assignment. This assignment helps students identify those aspects of writing that distinguish that writing as effective or ineffective. In completing this assignment, students often find that many of the characteristics of good mathematical writing are those they're used to seeing in good writing in other disciplines.

Another useful assignment is the one I call the "Watchword" exercise. This exercise is given to students in a course introducing students to rigorous mathematical proofs. Each student is given a single word or phrase with a familiar nonmathematical meaning that is used frequently (and more carefully!) in mathematics. The student must then write a short analysis of that word or phrase, explaining its usage both in everyday language and in technical discourse, providing examples to illustrate both.

Some of the words included in the exercise surprise the students at first. Consider the word *whenever*. For students used to writing casual phrases like "I'll do that whenever I want to," it is hard to recognize in saying "A function is continuous whenever it is differentiable" we are conveying a very specific logical fact. Namely, if a mathematician writes "*Y* whenever *X*" she claims unequivocally that the statement *X* logically implies the statement *Y*: *Y* is a necessary consequence of *X*, in every instance.

After completing a draft explanation of their watchwords, students exchange their drafts and perform out-of-class reviews of one another's work. I ask them to focus their reviews on their peers' description of the divergence between the words' everyday meanings and their technical meanings. The reviews help students make this divergence as clear as possible.

The Watchwords exercise serves several important learning goals. In writing about the words they've been given, students learn to apply these words carefully and only when called for. They learn to recognize the subtle differences between the meanings of distinct technical words and phrases. Moreover, I have found that the exercise makes students more conscious about their choice of words when writing in other disciplines and more conscious about the audience for whom they're writing. "This assignment helped my writing outside of math, too," reported one student after completing the assignment. "I think really carefully now about what words like 'if' and 'or' mean whenever I use them."

The Watchwords exercise is adaptable to nearly any discipline. A statistician can ask his students to define *sample, population,* or even the deceptively simple *average.* A physicist can focus on terms like *force, mass, flux,* or *momentum*; and a computer scientist on *gate, cloud, semaphore,* and *tree.* A brief reflection on the language you use every day in your discipline will yield you a list of words and phrases you can analyze in your own courses.

LEARNING LOGS

Much like journals, which we encountered in the previous chapter, learning logs give students a place to reflect on their mastery of course concepts, but they may do so in a more strongly structured way. By explicitly tying students' writing in a learning log to their completion of problem sets or other homework, an instructor can get a snapshot of students' learning processes as they do their work and correct conceptual mistakes as they arise. Furthermore, much like day-books (also described in Chapter Four), learning logs give students a place to synthesize disparate ideas as their own ideas take shape. As an unnamed faculty member quoted in Melzer (2003) puts it, "A learning log is more than a personal journal or documentation of work done, it is a tool to help you integrate your thoughts on your course work, readings, research efforts, and personal experiences" (p. 101).

Angelo and Cross (1993) give tips for guiding students' conceptual development through learning logs. Audet, Hickman, and Dobrynina (1996) describe the use of learning logs in physics courses, and Baker (2003) describes a successful application of learning logs in the specific setting of an information security course. McIntosh and Draper (2001) show that learning logs can prove effective in math classes, too. As yet another example, let's take a look at the way a pair of my colleagues in mathematics use learning logs during an intensive summer preparatory program they help to run at their school.

For the past few summers, Matthew Haslam and Roberto Pelayo of the University of Hawai'i-Hilo (UH-Hilo) have run a summer program helping students transition successfully from high school mathematics classrooms to college math coursework. Pelayo notes that the majority of the students their school serves commonly use Pidgin English in day-to-day speech; this variety of English does not typically provide the specificity necessary to detail the precise mathematical definitions and relationships. Obviously this shortcoming can prove an obstacle in communicating math effectively.

In response, Haslam and Pelayo have begun to use ungraded learning log exercises to help students in the summer program learn to use language more clearly and more precisely. The learning log questions ask the students to respond qualitatively, rather than quantitatively, to various computational exercises, inferring patterns from the data they've found and drawing conclusions based on those patterns and data. Because this sort of pattern finding is the essential hallmark of mathematical abstraction, students are using their log entries to help learn to think like mathematicians.

Pelayo points out some of important learning habits the students develop through responding to the learning log questions. One of these, "bottom-up learning," is typified by a problem set appearing about a week and a half into the summer workshop. This problem set is designed to guide students' discovery of the effect on the graph of a given function of replacing "x" by "$-x$" inside of the function. In the learning log questions, the students are led to reflect on the effect they witness in their computations, comparing that effect with the effect they had seen on other functions in class. Pelayo notes the overall effect of the exercise: "We like this example because it highlights the role of the learning log in the workshop. Students are given sample computations, which they then use to construct a larger, more general pattern or relationship. Of course, the questions themselves hint at what the relationship should be. However, the students having to explain how they arrived at this broader relationship in written prose has a remarkable impact on their 'ownership' of the material. This is what Matt [Haslam] and I call *bottom-up learning*—where students take their own examples and use this to construct a broader theory" (2010).

Furthermore, Pelayo notes that as the teaching assistant responds to each learning log on a daily basis, "a dialogue of sorts emerges, reinforcing the notion that discourse has an appropriate place in Mathematics." In this way students learn that it's okay to question the ideas they learn, and that dialogue, discussion, and even disagreement are appropriate ways to get at the substance of math.

The learning logs have been so effective that Pelayo's colleagues are beginning to experiment with their use in other disciplines. One of Pelayo's students, Ashlee Kalauli, has written a series of learning log questions to accompany the problem sets assigned in UH-Hilo's intensive summer workshop in chemistry. The success of the learning logs in the UH-Hilo summer programs is particularly encouraging, for it demonstrates how this exercise can address linguistic difficulties as well as mathematical ones. Although writing instruction for second-language learners is beyond the scope of this book, it is clear that there is overlap between the sets of issues facing second-language learners and those facing students in the quantitative disciplines.

STUDENT-AUTHORED EXAM QUESTIONS

As practitioners of our disciplines we are all aware that pushing our understanding forward requires not only that we be able to answer critical questions about our disciplines but that we be able to ask those questions in the first place. Likewise, while students gain from answering the questions we put to them on exams and other assignments, they can gain just as much, or more, from crafting their own questions.

In asking students to take part in the construction of course material, we encourage them to become active authors of disciplinary knowledge. They deconstruct the ideas of the discipline, analyze them, question them critically, and reconstruct them. Crafting questions of appropriate difficulty and focus requires deep reflection on the concepts on which the questions are based. Often students must learn to think inductively, when previously they were asked only to think deductively, and to synthesize, when previously they were asked only to analyze. They become more keenly aware of the audience for which they are writing, as they must ensure the questions they come up with are neither too simple nor too complex. All of these skills help students become both better writers and better thinkers.

Roughly a week and a half before an exam is to be given, have a brief discussion with the students about the characteristics of a good exam question. How involved should such questions be? What sort of challenges should they present? Given the chance, students will often identify the same characteristics of good exam questions that we would name. Ask each of the students to write one question she feels is suitable for inclusion on the exam. Ideally, the questions they come up with should not simply be computational ones. For instance, they should not simply be multiple choice or short-answer questions. Rather, the questions' solutions should involve some interpretation and subtle application of course concepts. Each student should also write a model solution to her question and should indicate what about that solution makes it desirable.

After students have been given a day or two to craft their questions, hold an in-class peer review session. (Students who have not prepared questions should not be permitted to participate in the review.) First, give time for the students to trade their questions and solutions with partners and discuss both thoroughly. During their discussions the students can focus on the appropriateness of the questions they are reviewing: Are they suitably difficult and suitably involved? Can they be completed in the time allotted for the exam? Students can also focus on the solutions offered by the questions' authors: Do the solutions meet whatever criteria you've established for high-quality work in your course? Can the solutions be improved? How? In whatever time remains, the students can take turns sharing with the whole class the questions and solutions they have developed. At this point the students get further feedback on the work they've done. Besides offering additional peer review, this sharing also gives students a chance to review the material treated by the upcoming exam.

Give students another day to affect further changes to their questions and solutions, and then collect the final drafts. If possible, respond to them and return them to their authors before the exam is given. This will give you the chance to correct any errors you find so that students do not enter the exam with any critical misconceptions. If you ask the students to submit their work electronically, you may consider compiling the questions and solutions into a single list and sharing it with the class on a course website.

Making this exercise work takes some careful timing. You'll need to begin the exercise early enough for students to perform the review and revision, but not so early that the students' questions give an inaccurate picture of the concepts to be treated by the exam. The following schedule shows how you might arrange the activities in a class that meets three days a week:

- Monday: Students craft questions and solutions.
- Wednesday: In-class peer review is held.
- Friday: Final drafts of questions and solutions are due.
- Monday: Corrected drafts are returned to the students.
- Wednesday: Exam is given.

Of course, you may make the peer review an out-of-class activity, or omit it altogether, and students will still benefit from the exercise. However, including the peer review increases the students' awareness of, and engagement in, an effective writing process.

Including questions the students have written adds authenticity and urgency to the assignment: students are likely to craft their questions with more care when they know they may be used in the exam. I've had success including a single student-authored question on each exam, reserving several others for use as review questions. Green (1997) gives more ideas on how to use students' questions. The sample rubric in Table 5.1 may give you some ideas as to how to respond to the questions students come up with.

Let's close this section with a few discipline-specific examples that show how the exercise may look.

- *For a first-semester calculus course.* "Please design a practical problem dealing with kinetics that would be suitable for inclusion on our final exam. Your problem should have at least two (related) parts and meaningfully involve

Table 5.1

Sample Rubric for Assessing Student-Authored Exam Questions

Criterion	Not Met	Partially Met	Fully Met
Student's demonstrated understanding of the concepts being tested by the question	Student's understanding is absent or lacking	Student's understanding is more solid but may be incomplete	Student's understanding is clear, complete, and error-free
Difficulty level and elaboration of the question	Question is either too easy or difficult, or its solution demands only superficial understanding	Question demands more than superficial understanding, though may still be too brief or lengthy	Question is appropriately challenging and fitting in its length and level of elaboration
Quality of the student's solution	Solution is incorrect, unclear, or incomplete	Solution is mostly correct and complete, though there may be minor errors and parts may be hard to follow	Solution is clear, comprehensive, and error-free

each of *position, velocity,* and *acceleration.* Your problem should involve a real-world application and not simply refer to a 'particle in motion.' Please be sure that your problem is appropriately difficult yet not so challenging that it could not be solved in a reasonable amount of time (ten to fifteen minutes, for example). Finally, please provide a clear, complete, and correct solution to the problem you construct."

- *For a physical chemistry course.* "Please design a problem in which valence bond theory must be applied in order to analyze the structure of a simple molecule. Your problem should make clear what properties of the molecular structure the solver must determine. Please provide a clear, complete, and correct solution to the problem you construct."

- *For an abstract algebra course.* "Please design a problem dealing with groups whose solution requires the solver to understand the concepts of *subgroup, normal subgroup,* and *coset.* Your problem may be either abstract or concrete in flavor. Please provide a clear, complete, and correct solution to the problem you construct."

"GREAT DEBATES"

Few assignments I've found for quantitative classrooms help students develop awareness of the human element of the mathematical sciences as much as those I call "Great Debates." As students complete the steps of these lengthy assignments, they are asked to study carefully the ways in which various quantitative ideas first came to light. The students learn about the history of those ideas to understand the ideas' relationships to one another. Moreover, the students learn about the human inventors or discoverers of those ideas to understand the way those ideas have come down to us. Seeing the human side of scientific discoveries helps students to recognize their own potential as authors of knowledge, significantly bolstering their confidence.

The Great Debates assignments involve experiential components as well as written ones, but the two play together so well that it is difficult to separate them. Let's take as an example "*Newton v. Leibniz,*" a project I have included in my first-semester calculus course. This project takes several weeks to complete, and its successful completion requires the collaborative efforts of an entire class of roughly twenty-five to thirty students. The goal of the class as a whole is to stage a mock civil trial between the two generally recognized "discoverers" of calculus, Isaac Newton and Gottfried Leibniz. Though the two never faced each other in the courtroom, Newton did accuse Leibniz of plagiarizing his work. By the project's end, the students will decide whether or not they think Leibniz was guilty of this charge.

In order to stage a convincing trial, each of a dozen teams of three or four students prepares to fulfill a particular role during the assignment. Students play every part, including

- Judges and members of the jury
- Newspaper reporters who must write a "public" account of the project's proceedings
- Historical and mathematical experts who may be asked to testify as witnesses

- Colleagues of the two great mathematicians
- The litigants themselves, each teamed up with his respective attorneys

Each student will help to complete three writing assignments during the course of the project, written in the voice of one of these players.

Role Proposals

The first writing assignment comes at the project's beginning. After I have divided the students into the teams in which they will work, I ask the members of each team to write a brief proposal, indicating which two of the roles listed they would most like to play during the next several weeks. Each proposal should indicate clearly why the students prefer these roles to the others, and why they feel they would be able to fulfill those roles more effectively than their peers. These are persuasion papers the students are writing, and their persuasiveness is critical, for the most persuasive writers tend to get the roles they ask for.

Writing in Character

Once the roles have been assigned, one role per team, the students set to work on the next stage of the project. Each team's task (and next writing assignment) will differ according to the role the team has been given. For instance, below is the prompt I give to the "colleagues of Newton" and the "colleagues of Leibniz":

> Each team of colleagues will submit a letter of support for their respective colleague, indicating any evidence, mathematical or historical, they feel is relevant to the case at hand. The letter should take the form of a co-authored persuasive narrative in which each party to the letter offers his own evidence and support. It might work best if each individual colleague pens her or his own portion of the letter, but the letter should be "smoothed" out so that it reads as a single cohesive document. In order to add authenticity to your writing, feel free to write in the voice of the colleague as he comes to his friend's defense.

Meanwhile the litigants' legal teams must write up a summary of the legal arguments they will bring to court, the teams of expert witnesses must write a detailed account of the historical and mathematical details of the debate, and the teams of newspaper reporters go from team to team, gathering the data they will need to write a series of articles on the developing trial. After a week's time each team submits a rough draft to me, to which I respond with minimal marking (see Chapter Three). At the end of the following week, the students take part in an in-class "pretrial deposition" during which they share their work with opposing teams as though they are disclosing legal evidence. Not only does this activity add to the authenticity of the trial atmosphere; it also serves as a sort of peer review session giving the students yet one more chance to get feedback on their written work. On the day the trial is enacted in class, the students submit the final drafts of their second written assignments, for which each student on a given team will ultimately receive the same grade. Immediately following the trial, they begin work on the third written assignment.

Reflecting

The last piece of writing students complete is a brief reflection paper each student writes individually. Here I ask students to reflect on any aspect of the assignment, including the historical, mathematical, or philosophical issues it treats. I encourage students to raise their own questions if they wish and to answer those questions if they can. Above all else, I want their reflections to be personal and probing.

As the students' responses to this prompt generally make clear, projects like "*Newton v. Leibniz*" help students to discover the human side of mathematics. In their reflections students often write things like "Until this project I hadn't even heard of Leibniz, and I definitely hadn't heard of any kind of argument about who discovered calculus," or "I just kind of always thought that math was just handed down to us from textbook to textbook. I mean, I knew that wasn't really the case, that somewhere someone had to have come up with it, but I didn't give any thought to the kind of thinking and exploration and invention that went into creating it." It's clear from these kinds of comments that projects like this one help students to inculcate skepticism, to better understand the nature of scientific discovery and progress, and to perceive their own potential as authors of scientific knowledge. All of this is done without detracting from course content, for students learn a great deal about the basic disciplinary principles underlying the historical dispute as they complete the project.

Many other courses in quantitative disciplines lend themselves nicely to similar Great Debates, each with its own rich history and authentic drama:

- *For a course introducing mathematical proofs. Intuitionism v. formalism.* Students face off in the roles of David Hilbert and L.E.J. Brouwer, the dominant proponents of these two schools of mathematical logic.

- *For a modern physics course. Bohr v. Einstein.* Students replay the famous debates on quantum mechanics between these two giants of twentieth-century physics.

- *For a macroeconomics course. Keynes v. Friedman.* Students stage a mock debate between Milton Friedman and J. K. Galbraith as they compare the benefits and costs of the Keynesian and monetarist economic theories.

WRITING FOR LAY AUDIENCES

The Great Debates assignment asks students to assume the role of one or another character and to write for a particular audience. Awareness of personal voice and awareness of audience are two of the most important skills a writer can develop, no matter the field in which she is writing. Often the audience for whom we ask our students to write is a tech-savvy one, consisting of their class peers, their professors, or some unidentified numerically literate other. If we ask our students to adjust their language to communicate with a "lay" audience, we challenge them to examine and explain key concepts from new points of view. Moreover, this skill is a critical one for students in quantitative disciplines to cultivate, as many of them will pursue careers in areas in which communicating with a nontechnical audience is essential. (See Kantrowitz, 1985; Keane & Gibson, 1999; Lehman, 1979; and Linte, 2009, for some hints on helping students write technically for lay audiences.) I consider a concrete example here.

My colleague Charles James, a professor of chemistry, challenges his students to adjust to a new audience through writing assignments in his first-year seminar course titled "Bad Science Fiction." These assignments ask students to identify the ways in which science fiction films violate scientific principles and then explain these violations to an interested party. The final product of one such assignment, which James calls "A Lucas Letter," is a letter addressed to director George Lucas, advising him on the technical aspects of his remake of a classic Japanese science fiction film.

James takes care to guide his students through the writing process as they craft their letters. As a first step the students read the American Association for the Advancement of Science's Benchmarks for Science Literacy Online (available at http://www.project2061.org/tools/benchol/bolintro.htm). The students then write a brief reflection on the benchmarks for science literacy for high school students. In their reflections, a sort of prewriting, the students create a list of things high school students should know about the physics involved in the science fiction film *Gamera the Invincible,* which the students have recently watched in class. This assessment helps them better understand the scientific literacy of the audience they will be addressing in their letters.

The students next meet in class to discuss their reflections. Each student emerges from the discussion with one scientific principle he will address in his letter to Lucas and a few examples of that principle's violation in the original film. During the next week the student writes a rough draft of the letter, which must advise Lucas on how to adjust his film so that it no longer violates the principle the student has selected. The students then subject their drafts to peer review in class. (See Chapter Three for some suggestions on how to make such peer review work effectively.)

In addition to helping students develop an accurate understanding of the work that goes into writing technically for a nontechnical audience, it also draws their attention to the writing process. There are many ways to vary this assignment by asking students to adapt their discourse to different audiences. Here are some discipline-specific examples; I am sure you will have no trouble in coming up with your own. (See also Bean, 1996, and Phillips & Crespo, 1996.)

For a mathematical finance course. "You have been retained as a consultant to an investment firm hoping to invest in a fictitious start-up whose portfolio is described in the documents available on the class website. Half of you have been chosen to support the investment, and half of you have been chosen to oppose it. Write an investment report addressed to the executives of the firm in which you defend your position on the investment. Keep in mind that the executives may not be as versed in the mathematical details of the portfolio as you are."

For an atmospheric thermodynamics course. "The magazine *Scientific American* has asked you to write a guest article on the role of convection in determining climate and weather. Your article must be at least 1,000 words, but no more than 2,000 words, long. Your audience consists of scientifically curious readers who are not necessarily familiar with the technical aspects of the physics behind convection."

For a number theory course. "In 2004 it was proven that it is possible to test the primality of a number in polynomial time. Given how easy it is to understand prime numbers, the public received the proof with interest, despite the complexity of the proof itself. Write an article for the *New York Times* newspaper in which you describe the basic idea of the proof without getting into the proof's technicalities. Your article must be between 500 and 1,000 words long."

STUDENT-AUTHORED TEXTBOOKS

It's very easy for students in quantitative disciplines to become passive receivers of knowledge. Our disciplines depend heavily on formulas, functions, and theorems, and our students spend much of their time simply memorizing these data without being asked to make sense of them in context. It's easy for students to feel as though they lack agency or control over their learning. Students stand to gain much greater understanding of the concepts their courses treat if they are asked to become the authors, quite literally, of that understanding. This is exactly what the student-authored textbook assignment demands of the students as they work together to contribute to a single "textbook" for the course. Like most "real" textbooks in quantitative disciplines, the students' textbook will contain explanations of key course concepts as well as visual aids, examples, and exercises as appropriate.

This project as I describe it here is lengthy, spanning the entire length of a given semester. The book takes shape chapter by chapter as new ideas are addressed in class, each chapter addressing a few weeks' worth of course material. However, the project is easy to scale back. For instance, instead of crafting a "textbook," students could craft less lengthy "study guides" or other supplementary materials for the various units of their course. Alternatively, students could spend a week or two at the semester's end putting together a *Cliff's Notes* version of the entire course.

Like the projects outlined in the previous two sections, this project is completed in successive stages, each one readying the students to begin work on the next. Here I lay out the project as I've assigned it in several intermediate and upper-level classes, including an introduction to proofs course, a topology course, and a linear algebra course.

Brainstorming

Most of the work on the textbook is done chapter by chapter. The first step in preparing a given chapter is to brainstorm a list of topics the chapter will address. I typically take ten or fifteen minutes of class time to complete this task, which must be done once every three weeks or so. I ask each student to spend five minutes coming up with her own list of topics for inclusion before opening the matter up to a full-class discussion. By the end of ten minutes' time the students should have a list of roughly eight to ten topics. During the next week the students will work in teams of two to four in drafting "sections" of the textbook dealing with the topics we have identified. I typically assign students to each section randomly, but you may consider assigning students to teams in such a way that their strengths and weaknesses complement one another.

Initial Drafts

During the next week the students work on their sections on their own time. I encourage the students to combine intuitive explanations with formal definitions and to use their own voices as they try to make clear the concepts they're writing about. I also encourage them to supplement their exposition with examples and exercises whenever necessary and to include appropriate diagrams, graphs, and other visual aids. Although they are given no formal parameters regarding length or format, I've found that students typically write one to three typewritten pages on each section assigned to them.

This assignment would be tremendously difficult to manage if the students did not type their contributions to the textbook and exchange their drafts electronically. Obviously this requires that students become proficient at typesetting their work, and this alone poses difficulties in those disciplines that use special symbols and notation. Most, if not all, of the students enrolled in the courses in which I've assigned the textbook project either had previously learned to use the LaTeX typesetting language (about which I say a few words at the end of this chapter) or were learning to use it at the time of the assignment.

Editorial Review Sessions

In a week's time I collect drafts of the sections completed by the individual teams (one draft per team) and assemble them into a single portfolio. The next task the students face is performing an initial review of one another's work. To do this the students meet informally in roughly hour-long sessions outside of class. They meet in a common area with the entirety of the current chapter in front of them. I try to schedule two or three review sessions so that all students have an opportunity to take part in at least one review session for each chapter, and I require students to take part in a certain number of review sessions in order to receive full credit for participation in the course. However, in my experience that compulsion is hardly needed: most students quickly realize how much their understanding benefits from taking part in as many sessions as they can, and participation is rarely an issue.

All students present at a review session take turns reading each of the sections submitted by their peers, making comments on the drafts that they read.

They ask questions of the others present and compare their comments with their peers'. During these sessions each student develops a deeper understanding of the topics treated by those sections she didn't write. Students also spend several minutes deciding the order in which the sections they've written should appear, and whether more work is needed to smooth the transitions from one section to the next.

Typically I am available for consultation during these review sessions, but I encourage students to mediate themselves whatever disputes they have regarding the textbook drafts. I intervene only if I discover that every student shares a common and critical misconception that requires correction.

Revising, Reiteration, and Final Editing   After a week's worth of review sessions, I return the commented drafts to the teams of students who crafted them. During the next week, on their own time, the students perform revisions that have been suggested to them before submitting the revised drafts to me for safe-keeping. At about this time the cycle will be starting anew, with a new chapter's worth of topics brainstormed, divvied up, written about, and discussed.

At the semester's end, the students gather for a final round of review sessions. These last sessions focus not on the draft sections of a single chapter but rather on the revised versions of every chapter considered as a whole. With the entire project laid out before them, the students can attend to broader compositional concerns. They can adjust the transitions from chapter to chapter in order to make their work read smoothly from start to finish. They can eliminate redundancy in their exposition and identify those places where that exposition could be made more clear. They can detect and correct errors in their arguments and computations, and they can determine where further examples may be needed in order to clarify the points they are trying to make.

At this point in the process I often lend a hand in the editing process, as by now the project has grown so unwieldy as to preclude large-scale revision by any single student. I ask the students to submit all of their electronic files to me once the chapter-by-chapter edits are complete, and I then help the students make whatever editorial changes they have indicated for the work as a whole. The finished product is often impressive in its scope and length, on the order of sixty or seventy pages. The students are always astounded at both the quality of their collaborative work and the immensity of the project they've completed. Because of the project's highly collaborative nature, no single individual, neither student nor instructor, performs a back-breaking amount of work in completing this project. I would estimate that I spend little more than a dozen hours on the project over the course of the entire semester.

In many ways this assignment is the ultimate writing-to-learn activity. In completing the assignment the students are doing far more than simply reiterating the ideas they talked about in class. In order to develop the mastery of these ideas needed to explain them to their peers, the students are examining the ideas closely and interrogating them. They are making decisions about how these ideas fit together and follow from one another. They are making decisions about the best way to illustrate these ideas through formal notation, visual aids, and logical arguments. The students are generating their own examples and exercises, demonstrating the extent to which they have become authors of their own knowledge. For this project, writing is more than a means of expression; it is a means of learning.

This project may not be appropriate for every class. It works best in smaller classes, with no more than twelve to fifteen students; involving many more students than this makes the project unmanageable. Furthermore, the project works best when the concepts the textbook will treat are not inaccessibly abstract. Students will have great difficulty offering anything other than pre-made examples and parrot-like paraphrasing of technical definitions in very abstract courses. This was the problem I encountered in attempting the textbook activity in my course on topology, in which students had a hard time putting very abstruse ideas into their own words.

GRANT WRITING

Many of us are accustomed to seeking financial support for our research or other academic efforts, and so for us the genre of the grant proposal is a familiar one. Although few of our students will have occasion to write grant proposals as undergraduates, many of those who plan on pursuing careers in the quantitative disciplines will someday find grant writing a useful skill.

Moreover, there are many aspects of grant writing that make writing a grant proposal a very healthy exercise for all students. For instance, writing a grant proposal is ultimately an exercise in persuasion, in which the purpose, the audience, and the tone of the writing expected are very clearly defined. Grant-funding agencies have very explicit criteria by which the proposals they receive will be evaluated. Students are therefore challenged to meet those criteria through their writing. Finally, grant-funding agencies make use of their own peculiar watchwords: anyone who's written a proposal to the National Science Foundation knows well what is meant by the terms *intellectual merit* and *broader impacts*. Therefore to write a successful proposal, students must learn to make effective use of appropriate terminology.

To make grant writing a meaningful academic exercise, it's important to make the assignment relevant to the course material. Grant-writing assignments take on much greater authenticity in courses with clearly defined service learning components or other avenues for community engagement. Courses in which students involve themselves with outside organizations or civic agencies, or courses in which students are asked to examine and act on public policy decisions, offer the ideal setting for grant writing.

My colleague Samuel Kaplan teaches such a course in our department. Through the course, titled "Social Justice and Math," Kaplan strives to heighten students' awareness of the effects mathematical literacy has on people's lives. According to the course's catalog description, "The course explores the notion of numeracy (math literacy), the value of numerate citizens as well as the economic and political dimensions of numeracy. We approach this topic using primary sources, secondary scholarly sources, popular media and service learning. . . . By the end of the semester, students should be able to demonstrate a working knowledge of key issues of numeracy and society"(UNC Asheville Spring 2011 class schedule)."

A few weeks into the course Kaplan assigns a grant-writing exercise in which students are asked to lay out plans for a project that will affect societal change through increased mathematical literacy. A successful proposal will be one that addresses at least two of the four philanthropic goals of the fictitious funding agency. These goals, adapted from criteria established by the Bill & Melinda Gates Foundation (www.gatesfoundation.org), are as follows:

1. Help reduce inequities in society
2. Produce measurable results
3. Catalyze sustainable change
4. Collaborate with government or not-for-profit partners

In addition to addressing these goals, students' proposals must adhere to rigid mechanical and structural specifications not unlike those mandated by real funding agencies. These specifications constrain everything from the font size to the broad organization of the proposal, which must include, for example, explicit discussions of the project's objectives, methods, assessment, and budget.

Once submitted, the students' proposals are subjected to peer review. A group of students reviews each grant and, with the help of a performance list Kaplan provides to them (shown in the textbox), decides whether or not the proposed project is worthy of funding. To give his students some practice at applying the review criteria before this peer review he brings in snippets from his own grant proposals. He indicates that this "practice peer review" helps both to establish inter-rater reliability and to expose the students to helpful examples of language and organization they could incorporate into their own proposals.

PEER REVIEW EVALUATION SHEET FOR GRANT PROPOSALS

The group must produce a document of 200 to 350 words summarizing the strengths and weaknesses of each project. One copy will be turned in to the student and a second copy will be turned in to the professor. You will evaluate the grant on the following guidelines:

Conformity (pass/fail: Do not proceed with evaluation of proposal if these criteria are not met):

- Each section is separate.
- Each section is the proper length.
- The font is correct.
- The borders are all at least one inch.
- The proposal seeks no more than $15,000.
- The proposal is virtually free of grammatical and spelling errors.

Purpose (out of 10 points): The proposal addresses math literacy with a targeted group.

Meets grantor's goals (out of 30 points): The proposal must meet at least two of the following:

- Help reduce inequities in society
- Produce measurable results
- Catalyze sustainable change
- Collaborate with government or not-for-profit partners

(continued)

Clarity (out of 30 points)

- The ideas expressed are clear.
- The problem is stated and supported.
- It is clear how the proposal can be implemented.
- The program can be adapted if the situation alters.

Efficacy (out of 20 points)

- The proposed assessment is feasible.
- The idea can be reproduced in other locations.
- The project can be carried out with the identified resources.

Budget (out of 15 points)

- The budget reflects ideas in the proposal.
- The expense justifications are reasonable.
- The sum of the items is correct.

As you might suspect, the students' proposals vary greatly in quality and sophistication. "Some are quite lousy, while others are nearly ready for submission," Kaplan indicates. Many of the proposals focus on activities in the students' own experience and propose professional development for tutors and staff at community centers. Others request funds to secure resources like computers, games, and other educational materials. More ambitious grant writers go to great lengths, interviewing local "experts" (teachers, tutors, community leaders) in order to lend credence to their proposals. Some students have told Kaplan they would have liked to have had the chance to actually submit their completed proposals. "They did a lot of work," Kaplan noted, "and they said that in the future if they were to do that much work, they would want it to count for something."

Others of Kaplan's students had just this chance. Students in his first-year seminar course titled "Math and Society" were asked to write proposals for a one-day event that would improve math literacy in the community. Kaplan recruited me and two upper-level math majors to assist him in reviewing the students' proposals. The student whose proposal was judged most promising was given $200 out of the

Math Club student activities fund to carry out the proposed activity publicly on "Pi Day," March 14. Knowing that the winning proposal would be implemented helps the students approach the assignment with considerable urgency. What could have simply been an academic exercise was transformed into one with tangible extrinsic rewards.

Many local businesses have a stake in improved math and science education, and these businesses may be willing to offer modest funding to promising grant proposals authored by students in quantitative disciplines. The same is true of a number of community organizations, private foundations, and local, state, and federal governmental agencies. Your university's foundation office may be able to help you find potential partners in your community should you wish to make this assignment an authentic one. Kiefer and Leff (2008) offer more ideas for what they call "client-based" writing opportunities, which include genres such as brochures, magazine articles, and website content, the last of which we turn to now.

WIKIS AND OTHER WEBSITES

A *wiki* is a collection of interlinked websites, typically written and edited by the wiki's users. The first wikis were formed just over a decade ago, and since then thousands more have been founded. Some, like the famous Wikipedia (www .wikipedia.org), contain information on an enormous variety of topics. These wikis represent the combined work of tens of thousands of collaborators and are visited daily by millions of users. Other wikis treat more specialized topics and may not be open to all. Many schools, companies, and community organizations maintain wikis to help their members and employees exchange information and draft collaborative documents.

Why not ask your students to develop a wiki addressing the information they learn in your course? (Payne, 2009, describes one such assignment in a computer science course focusing on electronic resource sustainability.) The way in which your students work on this wiki could be very similar to the way they would work on a student-authored textbook, at least at first. At the end of each unit of your course, ask students to brainstorm a list of items from that unit that they would like to include in the wiki. Each of these items may be little more than a term or a special symbol, but it could comprise a broad and complex concept that underpins the course. With this list of items in hand, you and your students can go about dividing up the work. For the next week, the students craft initial drafts of their wiki websites.

At the end of this time, instead of meeting for "editorial review sessions," the students review and revise one another's work online, as they would when working on any other wiki. This work can be done from their dorm rooms and apartments, and it can be done at any time of day. The online tools that support wiki creation will give you ways of monitoring the edits performed on every page, enabling you to keep track of each student's participation in the project. Unlike in the case of the textbook, there is no need for a "final editing," for the wiki will continue to evolve for the remainder of the course. Any single wiki website can be reviewed and revised over and over until the end of the term, and new websites will be linked to the old ones as they are created.

Having students create a wiki for your course helps students meet many of the same goals achieved by the student-authored textbook assignment. As in that assignment, students must assemble explanations, examples, and exercises to give their readers a full treatment of the course's key concepts. As in that assignment, the students will need to collaborate extensively in order to succeed in creating a complete and cohesive document.

However, there are differences between a textbook and a wiki. For instance, textbooks are typically read "linearly": even if the reader doesn't read the book from cover to cover, he usually reads section after section or chapter after chapter, in the order in which they're printed. On the other hand, wikis and other websites are built to be navigated in a nonlinear fashion. This means that students working on a wiki need not be as concerned about which topic must be placed before which others; instead they need to provide links from one page to another in the appropriate places. Moreover, much like the "maps" created through clustering (which we encountered in Chapter Two), wikis challenge students to recognize more complex interrelationships among the concepts they write about. Finally, composing on the Web requires greater attention to the layout of multiple text elements, and to the interplay between text and images, than is needed in most offline composition. This greater emphasis on visual rhetoric poses a new compositional challenge to students.

Wikis are not the only sort of website you can ask your students to create. Here are a couple of other ideas:

- *Tutorial website*. Ask your students to design a website whose purpose is to provide assistance to students who are struggling with key course concepts. Like a wiki, the website might include links to various student-authored websites dealing with those concepts, each illustrated with fully solved sample problems. It might also include links to outside websites that contain information relevant to the course.

- *Supplements or complements to other writing projects.* Many of the writing projects we have considered before can be augmented by including an online component.

  - Students can post the analyses of their "watchwords" on a single website as a reference for use throughout the course.

  - Students can compile all of the exam questions they have written, creating an excellent resource for reviewing for the exam.

  - Students can post new chapters of their student-authored textbook as those chapters are written, reviewed, and revised.

  - Students can design a homepage for the program or event to be funded by the monies supplied by the grant for which they've written a proposal.

Obviously, composition in Web media may require technical skills not normally expected of students. Unless your students have access to user-friendly Web design software, they may need to know the basics of HTML and JavaScript to create anything but the simplest websites. Students in some disciplines (like computer science) may acquire these skills in due course, but for many students learning these skills will require additional time and effort.

However, there are a number of free online Web design tools that can help your students design wikis and other websites. For example, PBworks (http://pbworks.com), Wiggio (http://wiggio.com), and even Google (http://sites .google.com) offer a variety of tools that help writers communicate and collaborate on shared documents. However, most of these resources fail to give users the means to include special notation and equations, limiting their usefulness in the quantitative disciplines. (See my comments on specialized typesetting software at the end of this chapter.)

CREATIVE WRITING PROJECTS

Students majoring in nonquantitative fields often come to our courses with hesitation, anxiety, or even fear. Think of the sociology major who has to complete a course on statistical methods, or the literature major who has to fulfill your university's core math requirement. These students are often scarred from their previous encounters with math-based courses and sometimes even have chosen their fields of study so that they can avoid further such encounters. For them, working with functions and formulas and other quantitative data can be terrifying.

Asking these students to engage mathematical ideas through creative writing in various genres can help to put them at ease. These students are often more familiar with novels, plays, and poems than they are with expository papers and technical reports. When they are offered the chance to write a poem about precalculus, or a children's book in which they make sense of certain basic physical or chemical principles, they often respond with redoubled effort and with delight.

Creative writing offers benefits to all students, not just to those who are anxious about math. The rich language of creative genres like drama and poetry, strikingly different from that of most quantitative disciplines, gives every student a new way of examining the concepts in our courses. Think of the familiar academic metaphor of the lens: new language offers a new lens through which to view the ideas we present to our students. This new lens can be a powerful one. It can help students see past dense notation and technical terminology to the intuitively simple ideas that lie at the heart of our fields. It can help students find new metaphors they can use to uncover connections among ideas whose relationships they'd overlooked before. (See Bahls, 2009, for further discussion.)

Moreover, creative writing can help students to gain confidence and overcome their trepidation regarding quantitative disciplines; confidence is critical factor affecting student success in these disciplines (Hackett & Betz, 1989; Hannula, Maijala, & Pehkonen, 2004; and Hembree, 1990). Creative writing allows students to use familiar language to help them make sense of unfamiliar ideas. It gives them a safe place where they can rest as they reflect on these unfamiliar ideas. "You may use any words you feel are appropriate," I remind the students as they begin their creative writing projects. "I only ask that you take the project seriously."

Poetry

Poetry can be a powerful means of expression in a wide variety of courses. Bahls (2009), Braga and Kantz (2010), Connor-Green and others (2006), and Samuels (1987) all give specific examples of the way poetry can appear in various disciplinary settings. Some scholars have even held up poetry as an effective tool for scholarship as well as teaching (Cahnmann, 2003; Glesne, 1997; Richardson, 1992, 2000).

I have assigned poetry-writing exercises in both precalculus and first-semester calculus courses. The assignments are open-ended ones that allow the students great latitude in choosing the topic and tone of their poems. Students are asked to write a single poem each, and each poem should involve mathematics in some fashion, whether as an element in the poem's structure or as the basis for the poem's content. Though some of the students use the assignment to write specifically about the ideas we discussed in class, many simply write about more general mathematical ideas or their personal engagement with those ideas. Even in these cases, when course content is not explicitly addressed, the time students spend on the exercise is time well spent, as it goes toward improving students' confidence in doing math.

Though these assignments call for students to write creatively, the assignments are structured to help students complete them in stages. Students are asked to submit rough drafts of their poems roughly a week before the final drafts are due. The comments I make on these drafts are designed to help the students think about tone and theme and word choice. I offer each student my impressions of the poem as written. I sometimes ask the student to confirm or question my impressions: "You seem to strike an angry tone here. Is this intended?" or "You appear to focus on the theme of 'fear.' What words might make this theme more apparent?"

Once I've returned the drafts to their authors, the students review one another's work and are invited to share their work with the whole class in a sort of "poetry reading." (This last step is not a compulsory one, as students are often uncomfortable sharing very personal writing with the class as a whole.) Students are invited to make further adjustments to their poems after this reading and before submitting their work. Each student must also submit a brief "analysis" of the poem in which he describes the choices he made as he crafted his poem (regarding word choice, structure, and so forth) and how those choices affect the poem's meaning.

It is trickier to grade the students' poems than it is to grade more conventional writing projects. Clearly correctness has no place in this assessment, and the other criteria I typically apply to written work are difficult to apply to the students' poems. Given the staggering spectrum of poetic styles, how can I tell if a poem is "complete," or even "well composed"? In the end, the analysis the students include with their final drafts helps me to see how much thought and effort the student has put into the project, and those students who have clearly dedicated a great deal of thought and effort are rewarded with high marks.

I've noticed two consistent learning outcomes of these exercises. First, through their poems students are often able to make better mathematical sense of the world around them, in effect applying their new knowledge in a real setting. One Calculus I student's collection of *haikus* included several poems meeting this goal. Poetry helped Katherine Clark, who later became a creative writing major, to see math in her everyday surroundings. She describes one of her encounters in her poem "Math in Daily Life":

> Patterns on my bunks,
> They resemble the graphs of
> Cosine and sine curves.

She questioned the nature of physical phenomena we dealt with in some of our in-class exercises, as in "Confusion":

> A tall ladder falls
> At twenty feet per second
> Why would it do this?

Finally, she even reflected on other writing assignments she'd completed in our course (see the earlier discussion of the *Newton v. Leibniz* project):

> Did Leibniz invent
> Calculus or did he steal
> The work of Newton?

Braga and Kantz (2010) give examples of similarly insightful poems by a student in an introductory chemistry course.

The second learning outcome is more affective. I've noticed that students use their poems to confront their feelings about mathematics and about doing math. Freed from having to use technical terminology, students felt safe to explore this affective aspect of their mathematical education using a wealth of more literary language. Amanda's poem, "Imperfect," speaks of the frustration she felt in working with others who weren't as ready to learn as she was:

> I am ready to be challenged
> Ironically this is the first thing which has been problematic
> It is difficult for me to be patient and understanding with others
> Irritation seems to be my main state of emotion

Intricate concepts are something I crave
Implicit differentiation as surprisingly stimulating
I fear my arrogance will be my downfall
I am ready to be challenged with others who feel the same way

When I quizzed her about the fact that every line of her poem begins with the letter *I*, Amanda admitted that she'd not intended this pattern at first, but once aware of it she saw it as a challenge to maintain it for the length of the poem. This repetition of the first-person singular pronoun makes the reader all the more aware of the highly personal nature of the poem. I was impressed at Amanda's ability to express such negative feelings as irritation and arrogance. In writing about these feelings Amanda was better able to dissipate them, or at least to be more aware of them so that she could work around them.

Other disciplines are equally open to poetical examination. Why not challenge students to write a poem in which they reflect on quantum mechanics or thermodynamics? Why not challenge them to write a poem patterned on the shape of a price curve, or on the structure of an atom's electron orbitals? As likely as not the poems your students write in response to these prompts will not stand out as works of literature. However, in playing with the meaning behind their poems and in picking out precisely the right words to use, your students will gain a good deal of insight into the ideas you're asking them to write about.

Other Creative Genres

Since many people are as intimidated by poetry as they are by math, it can comfort students to give them a range of creative genres with which to engage disciplinary ideas. My colleague Janine Haugh recognized this when she was asked to teach our department's precalculus course. Knowing that many students enroll in this course in order to satisfy the university's core mathematics requirement and most never take another math class afterward, Haugh recognized that precalculus students are rarely intrinsically motivated by the course material. Thus one of her goals was to get her students to engage course concepts creatively, to enliven them, and to inject them with excitement.

To do this she designed an assignment that asks students to examine precalculus concepts using a creative genre of their choice. "Let's see if we can develop a project where we can all let our interests shine through!" she begins. She then gives her students several project ideas.

PRECALCULUS CREATIVE PROJECT IDEAS

- Write a song about your favorite topic that we've covered so far.

- Write mathematical poetry (you may want to do an Internet search for *Oulipo*).

- Write a short story (or a long word problem) that makes use of a topic we have covered.

- Write a children's book that could be used to teach a precalculus topic to a young child.

- Create a video that could be used to teach a topic from this course to next semester's precalculus students.

- Develop a game that involves precalculus topics.

- Research a mathematical topic that interests you or a way to apply mathematics to your field. Summarize in a brief paper (with citations).

Though this assignment, like the poetry assignment, is nontraditional, it is still structured in such a way as to help students approach writing as a process and not a product. Haugh asks her students to submit a proposal one week into the project. Students are asked to make an appointment with her at some point during the following week to discuss their projects with her, one on one. At this time she can identify potential problems and offer formative feedback on the students' work.

The students' responses to this open-ended project were impressive. Their projects spanned the spectrum of ideas Haugh had suggested to them, including board games, murder mysteries, and more than one children's book. A page from one of these books, created by the student Kelsey LaQuerre, is shown in Figure 5.1. Here, Duke (an English sheepdog) narrates one of several steps a person performs in simplifying a complex fraction, while various other characters demonstrate the step in the background. LaQuerre's careful explanation in words is complemented exactly by the animals' actions, making this step of the process clear. It's obvious that in completing this project LaQuerre herself had to master the process she was describing.

Haugh remarked that students responded well to the opportunity to choose the medium in which they would work. That chance to choose empowered the

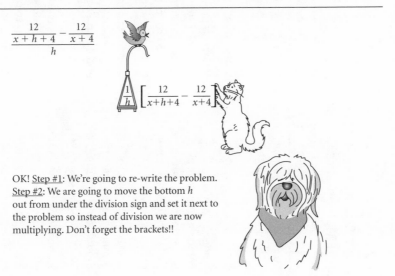

Figure 5.1
A Page from Precalculus Student Kelsey LaQuerre's
Children's Book on Simplifying Complex Fractions

$$\frac{\dfrac{12}{x+h+4} - \dfrac{12}{x+4}}{h}$$

$$\frac{1}{h}\left[\frac{12}{x+h+4} - \frac{12}{x+4}\right]$$

OK! Step #1: We're going to re-write the problem.
Step #2: We are going to move the bottom h
out from under the division sign and set it next to
the problem so instead of division we are now
multiplying. Don't forget the brackets!!

students. She also noted that the assignment was received particularly favorably by students who typically struggle in math courses, and these students gained both confidence and content mastery by working on their projects. The most difficult aspect of the assignment for Haugh was grading students' work. Understandably, she had a hard time deciding what criteria to apply to the projects, especially given their incredible variety. The sample rubric in Table 5.2 (whose levels of achievement could easily be translated into points or grade levels) may give some idea of the issues involved in evaluating such work.

There are many other excellent sources illustrating the use of creative writing in quantitative courses.

- *In chemistry.* Alber (2001) gives examples of ways to use principles from chemistry, and principal figures from the history chemistry, as the basis for a creative writing assignment. van Ryswyk (2005) describes an elaborate assignment in an instrumental methods course that culminates in a multimedia demonstration of a particular instrumental method, including a brief film and complementary documentation.

Table 5.2
Sample Rubric for Assessing a Creative Writing Project in an Introductory-Level Mathematics Course

Criterion	Not Met	Partially Met	Fully Met
Project fulfills goals articulated in the student's project proposal	Student's goals not met	Student's goals partially met	Student's goals fully met (or reasonable justification given for unmet goals)
Project demonstrates student's understanding of the mathematical concept(s) underpinning its crafting	Student's project demonstrates no (or poor) understanding of related concepts	Student's project demonstrates partial understanding, but some aspects of related concepts remain elusive	Student's project demonstrates solid understanding of related concepts (with only minor errors)
Project successfully communicates understanding of the mathematical concept(s) to others	Little or no attempt to communicate understanding to others is present	Student attempts to communicate understanding, though these attempts may be incomplete or awkward	Student communicates understanding clearly and comprehensively
Project shows student's effort to achieve literary or aesthetic merit (whether or not this merit is fully realized)	Student's work shows no or little effort (it is sloppy and hastily formed)	Student's work shows some effort (some care is taken in its crafting; improvements have been made on a rough draft)	Student's work shows considerable effort and attention to detail (it is polished; effort is made to ensure aesthetic appeal)

- *In computer science.* McDermott, Eccleston, and Brindley (2008) describe how drawing a parallel between writing a computer program and telling a story helped them to reach students in a first-year computer science course.

- *In economics.* Goma (2001) describes an assignment similar to Janine Haugh's, in response to which students in her survey of economics course crafted short stories, plays, interviews, and other creative pieces.

- *In various disciplines.* Connor-Greene and others (2006) list several dozen poems, prints, and designs created by students in biology, chemistry, operations research, abstract algebra, computer science, and civil engineering. This book also includes faculty reflections on the assignments leading to these creative pieces.

A WORD ON TECHNICAL TYPESETTING

The writing students perform in most traditionally writing-intensive courses is easily done using ordinary word processing software. However, writing a document with anything but the most basic mathematical content with such software is time consuming and difficult, and the result is often unattractive. For this reason students in the quantitative disciplines have long had to compose much of their writing by hand.

Professionals in the quantitative disciplines use specialized typesetting software, such as LaTeX, to help create attractive documents with math content. LaTeX allows the writer to compose in ordinary text by entering the text verbatim. The writer creates special mathematical characters and symbols using "macro" commands that are replaced with the appropriate characters when the writer compiles the text he has entered. For instance, the command "\pi" will be replaced with the Greek letter π, and the command "\int" will be replaced with the symbol "$\int$," denoting the operation of integration.

I strongly advise offering your students who are interested in learning LaTeX a chance to do so. In learning the software the writer faces a steep initial learning curve, but with practice the software becomes very easy to use. I've begun teaching LaTeX to the students in our department's course introducing students to mathematical proofs, and I require students to use it for various projects and problem sets. Most students are eager to learn to use the software, especially when they see how nicely their work appears when using it. Though fluency may come only after several years of regular use, students who use LaTeX frequently for their coursework are usually proficient by the end of a single semester and are soon able to craft convincing visual rhetoric.

Why use such software? Its benefits go beyond producing an attractive finished product. Although writing with LaTeX requires the students to put forth a little extra effort in composing their work, this effort forces them to reflect more carefully on their writing. During the few minutes it takes a student to typeset a complicated mathematical expression, he is actively pondering the meaning and appropriateness of every symbol he uses in that expression. Almost without exception my students report that this extra opportunity for reflection gives them more confidence in their understanding of technical terms and symbols.

I hope that the activities contained in the last two chapters have helped give you confidence as an instructor of writing in your discipline. Your role as a teacher of disciplinary writing is an important one, but its importance may be matched by other, related roles. Ultimately the success of writing in the disciplines demands that we reflect critically on our practices, that we document them, analyze them, and share them with others. Therefore we must be more than teachers of writing; we must also be scholars of writing in our disciplines, and champions who are willing to stand up for writing's place in our curricula. Our next, and final, chapter says more about these roles.

Shaping the Future of Writing in the Quantitative Disciplines

I have learned a lot about writing in the disciplines since I first made my calculus students write in response to poorly planned essay prompts. I've learned how to break assignments up into manageable steps and how to arrange those steps so that my students could engage in a coherent writing process. I've learned how to give students feedback that lets them know not just how well they've *done* in their writing but also how they're *doing* as the writing takes shape. I've learned how to use writing as more than a means of communicating. For me and my students, it is also a means of discovery, exploration, and reflection, even in my most quantitative classes.

In previous chapters I've shared some of what I have learned with you. I would like to spend the final pages in this book not looking behind, but ahead. What more is there to be said about writing? We have at our disposal an immense wealth of writing resources, even in our disciplines, those furthest removed from traditionally writing-intensive areas. However, as our areas are among the last to adopt writing across the curriculum (WAC) practices, we still have much work to do to improve our understanding of writing and the roles it plays in our disciplines.

Fortunately, the kind of work that remains is familiar to us, as it is much like the work we do as scholars in our own areas. Our scholarly work requires us to keep up with current findings in our fields and to adapt others' innovations so that they will work well for us. The process of adaptation frequently prompts the discovery of new ideas on our own that we can share with our colleagues, beginning the cycle over again. So it is with teaching writing. If we keep abreast of new ideas, adapt them to our own courses and classrooms, and document carefully what we do, we can share our innovations, experiences, and analyses of their effectiveness, contributing meaningfully to what is already known about writing in our disciplines.

My goal now is to say a bit about this process of invention and the directions in which we can grow as we continue to work on writing in our disciplines. After describing more fully the process just introduced, I consider the roles we instructors play in making WAC work. Specifically, I see three major roles for us. First, since we are the experts in our disciplines, no one is more qualified than we are to be *teachers* of disciplinary writing. Moreover, this same disciplinary expertise makes us the ideal *scholars* of this writing. Finally, we must be *champions* of disciplinary writing, working to overcome the resistance we encounter to writing in our fields from outsiders, from our students, and from ourselves.

PUSHING WRITING FORWARD

We are curious creatures, prone to mimicry and play. When we see another person do something intriguing, many of us are inclined to try it out for ourselves to see what happens. Most real-world experiments are not perfectly replicable, so when I try to do the same thing you've done, chances are good that my results won't be the same. The differences I see might then give me insight into the subject of my experiment, leading to new ideas that I can test with further experimentation. This was the case, for instance, when I tried assigning a poetry exercise to my calculus students. At first the exercise merely offered a new way of helping students play with mathematical ideas. Soon I noticed that many of the students used the medium to express their emotional engagement with mathematics, leading me to ask them what function the poetry played for them. I was delighted to find that for many students the poetry helped develop confidence and dissipate anxiety (see Bahls, 2009), and since then I've made poetry a part of several of my courses.

We do well to approach writing with the same sense of curiosity and play. If you keep up with current trends in writing and writing instruction, you'll never be at a loss for new ways to work writing into your courses. Your record of experiments with writing (and your reflection on that record) will then help others to generate ideas of their own. Moreover, this record and reflection can lead to the more careful and controlled experimentation with which we're more familiar.

Keep Up with New Developments

Keeping abreast of new ideas related to writing is nowhere nearly as hard as it once was. One of the difficulties the WAC movement faced in its early years was a lack of communication among its advocates. Since relatively few faculty had adopted WAC principles and practices, these faculty had not yet built up the network of conferences, publications, and other resources that define an academic community and make it easier for the members of that community to keep in touch.

There is no such difficulty today. Many journals are devoted exclusively to writing in the disciplines and writing-to-learn, and many more treat writing within specific disciplinary contexts. Among the periodicals devoted to writing across the curriculum are *Across the Disciplines*, *College Composition and Communication*, *The WAC Journal*, and *Written Communication*. These journals publish articles on every aspect of WAC, from assignment design and assessment to developing and delivering full-scale WAC programs. Moreover, many discipline-specific journals publish frequently on issues related to writing. The following periodicals are just a few of those that treat writing regularly.

- *CBE-Life Sciences Education*
- *Innovations in Teaching and Learning in Information and Computer Science*
- *International Journal of Engineering Education*
- *Journal of Chemistry Education*
- *Journal of College Science Teaching*
- *Journal of Economic Education*
- *Journal of Engineering Education*
- *Journal of Information Systems Education*
- *Journal of Mathematics Teacher Education*
- *Journal of Research in Mathematics Education*
- *Journal of Research in Science Teaching*

- *Journal of Statistics Education*
- *Research in Science Education*

These publications offer one way to stay abreast of writing trends. Several major conferences also give scholars in WAC and WID further opportunities to interact. The annual Conference on College Composition and Communication, sponsored by the National Council of Teachers of English, has served this role since 1950. More recently (in 1990) the biannual International Writing Across the Curriculum Conference got its start. Meanwhile, various regional Writing Centers Association Conferences and Writing Program Administrators Conferences offer more modest forums for airing ideas about writing. These conferences are all open to, and welcoming of, interdisciplinary voices. Still closer to our academic homes, a growing number of disciplinary conferences now feature special sessions on writing in the disciplines and writing-to-learn. For instance, every year for the past decade the national Joint Mathematics Meetings have featured sessions on writing in math, and similar sessions are held at national and regional professional meetings in statistics, computer science, physics, chemistry, and economics.

Internet resources complement these more traditional ones. The WAC Clearinghouse (www.wac.colostate.edu/) provides a rich assortment of resources on writing, including research databases, online access to several journals and e-books, and a substantial supply of writing activities suitable for all disciplines. The International WAC Network (www.wac.colostate.edu/network/) gives directors of WAC and WID programs, faculty teaching writing-intensive course, and other friends of WAC virtual meeting spaces and message boards. Several of the more well-established university writing programs maintain copious Web resources, including Purdue University's Online Writing Lab (www.owl.english.purdue.edu/) and George Mason University's Writing Across the Curriculum program (www.wac.gmu.edu/).

Adopt and Adapt

Keep reading on writing, and sooner or later you'll come across an idea that appeals to you. You'll read an article in *Across the Disciplines* or catch a talk at a meeting sponsored by your own professional society, and you'll think, "That'll work well for my students." Chances are good that whatever ideas you plan to adopt will need some tweaking to make them work given the content in your courses, the learning needs of your students, and your own teaching style.

Change is not inherently unhealthy, but as I've noted before, it's unwise to make dramatic changes all at once. I learned this through experience: in the linear algebra course I mentioned in the Preface to this book, I introduced journaling, reflective writing, and a lengthy multistage research paper, not to mention frequent low-stakes exercises, all in a single semester. I'd never assigned journals or reflective pieces before, and I'm sure that my inexperience showed, as my responses to student work were often clumsy and inconsistent.

It's wiser to move writing into your courses one or two steps at a time. After all, it's better that you employ a handful of writing activities comfortably and confidently than that you saturate your course with poorly planned projects that confuse your students, make more work for you, and end up reinforcing all of the negative feelings you all may harbor about writing. You might want to begin by introducing a few low-stakes exercises to your students one semester and a few more the semester after that. Depending on your learning goals for a particular course, you may stop here: not every course needs to be a writing-intensive one, although the more students write the more ready they'll be to explore and express themselves in your discipline.

Once you've grown comfortable assigning and responding to low-stakes writing, you can introduce one or two more elaborate writing assignments. Be intentional in the design of these assignments, and be responsive to your students' needs as they complete them. Don't be afraid to make changes in assignments that aren't yet optimal, even if this means making midcourse adjustments. (I can't think of a single assignment I've given that's not undergone some revision from one semester to the next.) Offer students ample time to complete the assignments, and offer yourself ample time to respond to them. You do well to remember that although your responses will grow more efficient and effective with practice, students in successive iterations of the same course begin their semester back where their peers in previous years did.

Document What You Do

There are only one or two courses I have taught often enough to be able to identify immediately the concepts students will struggle with most mightily. For example, I've taught first-semester calculus often enough to say with certainty that students in that class will have great difficulty with the technical definition of a limit. Yet I couldn't tell which of the hundreds of concepts students encounter in second-semester abstract algebra will prove most difficult to them, as I've only taught the course twice in ten years. To keep track of students' struggles, I'll leave notes to myself: "They'll have trouble here. . . . They'll need help coming up with examples of this. . . . They'll have a hard time visualizing that." Notes like this also help me keep in mind alternative computations and particularly clear explanations.

Similarly, it helps me to keep an archive of the writing tasks I assign to my classes. After all, good assignments are worth preserving. If an assignment works well once, chances are good that it will work well again, and it'll often work well in different contexts or courses. Archiving assignments is a terrific timesaver, for though it can take several hours or more to put together an effective assignment, it may take only minutes to adjust an existing one for a different course.

I've found it helpful to save students' responses to my assignments as well. These responses make perfect models for students completing later iterations of the same assignments. For this purpose, samples of weaker writing serve as well as samples of stronger writing. It's as helpful to know how *not* to do something as it is to know how to do it well. Samples showing various levels of mastery of disciplinary writing conventions help students learn to recognize mastery in their own work. Moreover, students' responses help me as much as they help my students. As I mentioned earlier, even when I teach the same course, with the same assignments, in back-to-back terms, I never fail to forget where my students encounter difficulties in their writing. A quick glance at my record of student responses reminds me of the pitfalls I might need to point out to my new students as they begin these assignments.

I also take the time to reflect on my assignments as I make them and modify them. How did students respond to my prompt? Did they respond as I expected them to, or did they misunderstand me? What does their misunderstanding tell me about my expectations for their writing at that point in the course? In noting what worked well, and what didn't work at all, with a given assignment, I can easily adjust the assignment the next time I give it.

Much of this reflection is private and remains unshared. Elsewhere I reflect openly. I journal about my teaching in a publicly available blog ("Change of Basis," http://changeofbasis.blogspot.com), and there I devote special attention to my efforts to teach writing. The blog serves as a record of hits and misses, almost the way a lab notebook serves as a record of an experiment. But the blog is more than this: it's also a forum where my students and colleagues can enter into a conversation with me about my teaching. The almost instantaneous feedback I get on my pedagogical practices helps me refine each activity almost as soon as it's done, making each iteration of a particular exercise or assignment more effective the next time around.

An example might help here. On March 24, 2010, I wrote a rather rambling blog post in which I mentioned how I had recently abandoned the student-authored textbook project (see Chapter Five) in the topology course I was teaching at the time. Though the project had been tremendously successful in my department's introduction to proofs course, several weeks into the topology course its results had been lackluster. I posed a possible reason for these results: "Many of the concepts were proving very difficult for the students to paraphrase, so that only a handful of the students were producing textbook submissions which were anything more than reiterations of my own course notes" (Bahls, "Wha . . . ? A new *post*!? (Complete with interrobang . . .)").

Within hours, two topology students who had helped craft the student-authored textbook written in the previous semester's proofs course commented on the blog post, corroborating my suspicions. As Scott said, "I feel like the abstractness of topology is slightly (at least) more elusive than foundations of math. In many cases, the formal definition really is about the easiest way you can acurately [sic] describe a concept. Attempting to reword concepts enough to be original sometimes led to chaotic sentence structure and lack of fluidity." Brian agreed: "In addition to all of that I find that the material in topology is simply more difficult to take in compared to 280 [my department's introduction to proofs course]. It's very definition heavy with super abstract ideas. This means more time spent on homework just figuring out how it all works. It's not impossible, just more involved. But that puts the textbook idea further out of reach."

This feedback led to further conversations about that particular assignment. These conversations helped me to understand that there's nothing inherently wrong with the assignment; it's simply not appropriate, as I'd originally conceived it, in every course. I've since used the assignment successfully in other courses, modified to account for students' mathematical level and experience with writing, as well as class size. Without the conversations my blog began, I would have had a much harder time adapting a valuable assignment from one course to another.

Share Your Ideas

At this point you may have managed to generate a few new ideas out of old ones, and it may be your turn to share those ideas with others. As I mentioned, many major conferences in the quantitative disciplines now feature panels or paper sessions addressing writing in the disciplines, and many conferences devoted to academic writing and composition and rhetoric feature sessions on writing in quantitative disciplines. Furthermore, dozens of periodicals publish writing-related scholarship ranging from simple descriptions of successful low-stakes writing exercises to large-scale assessments of departmental writing programs.

I don't mean to oversimplify research in rhetoric and composition. Anecdotal evidence simply cannot substitute for the careful quantitative and qualitative analyses that distinguish high-quality research in any discipline. However, as when we perform research in our own fields, offhand observations can lead to testable hypotheses worthy of more thorough investigation. Although we may not be familiar with the specific methods composition theorists and rhetoricians use in their work, our training in our own disciplines and our attention to exactitude and rigor can help make us able scholars of writing in our disciplines. We are particularly well suited to investigate several important questions about writing in our disciplines, which I mention later in the chapter.

That said, you need not engage in rigorous research in order to share your experiences with others. Other faculty in the quantitative sciences can benefit greatly simply from hearing whatever writing "success stories" you can tell them, as can writing professionals on your campus, like instructors of first-year writing and writing center staff. You can likely find an audience for your ideas without even leaving your own campus, and there's no need to organize a formal workshop to trade tips on writing with your colleagues in your department. For instance, many of the writing-to-learn (WTL) activities introduced in Chapter Four require minimal formal preparation or training, and the basics of these activities can be conveyed in five minutes. Hallway conversations and brown-bag lunches can give you further informal opportunities to talk with your department colleagues about the benefits of including writing activities in disciplinary courses. You can afford to think small, at least to start.

"Big picture" ideas, like programmatic assessment and curricular overhaul, though important, can wait. But if your department's colleagues are open to innovation, they may help you to identify departmentwide learning outcomes and means for making writing flow seamlessly from course to course in your department. Initiatives like these take time to implement. You'll do best to ease writing into your department's curriculum as slowly as you would ease it into one of your courses. For example, my university began implementing writing-intensive courses several years before my own department made our "Introduction to Proofs" course writing intensive. Several more years passed before we introduced required writing in our senior seminar course. In taking our time we have made sure that all department faculty are on board with the changes we've adopted and that we all see the value in the writing our students do.

TEACHERS, SCHOLARS, CHAMPIONS

As I mentioned previously, I believe we have three main roles to play as we do our work in disciplinary writing. Of course, we must be *teachers* of writing, helping our students to write well in our disciplines and helping them to use writing as a tool to learn. We must also be *scholars* of writing, asking and answering questions about writing as it relates to our fields. Finally, we must be *champions* of writing, modeling WAC principles to others and making a case that writing has a place in our classrooms. WAC principles dictate that, because we are the experts in our areas, no one can better play these roles than we can.

Our Role as Teachers

At the start of their college careers most of our students receive a semester or two of instruction in writing. In these first-year composition courses, they encounter a wide variety of genres and forms, conventions and styles, audiences, purposes, and tones. No one particular genre is privileged over any other as students develop college-level writing skills. At many schools students continue for another year or two as generalists, completing courses in an interdisciplinary "core" designed to round them out as thinkers before they choose a field to specialize in. Much of the writing they do in these courses is stereotypical and easily labeled: reflections, responses, and research papers. Our schools' writing centers, staffed by experts in rhetoric and composition, give students expert guidance in completing more fundamental writing tasks.

It's easy for us to box up first-year writing courses and stow them away in our English departments or dedicated writing programs. It's just as easy to leave generalized writing instruction to our colleagues in areas where writing has traditionally dominated, like literature and history. However easy it is to compartmentalize this early writing instruction, we must not forget that writing happens everywhere on our campuses, and in every year of each student's college career. This ubiquity of writing is essential, given that many students now come to college with truly deficient writing skills in need of substantial remediation. Writing across the curriculum, and writing across every year of college, can help these students develop solid writing skills.

However, a student may not encounter the sort of writing she expects to do during the course of her career until she chooses her major. From this point forward, although first-year writing instructors and writing center staff can offer us assistance, it is largely left to us, as experts in our disciplines, and therefore experts in disciplinary writing, to help our students with more specialized writing tasks. If we're to teach writing, and if we're to use writing as a teaching tool, we might as well do these things well.

In a sense, this entire book has been about teaching writing, so I will say little more on the matter here. Note that the inventive process described in this chapter's previous section offers us a way of helping ourselves to be better teachers. We can begin by reading up on best practices, adopting and adapting those practices, and trying them out in our own classes. Reflecting on our successes and failures will help us fine-tune our attempts the next time we make them, and with practice we won't fail to teach more effectively.

Finally, I encourage you to build a relationship with the writing professionals on your campus. If your school has a writing center, get to know its director. This person (and her staff and students) will be able to help you find a place for writing in your courses. Talk to the faculty who teach your school's first-year writing courses, and find out what your students learn in these classes. Knowing this information will help you set realistic goals for writing in your own courses. Rest assured that the conversations you have with these people will help them as much as they help you. Given the traditional divide between writing and the quantitative disciplines, without exception my colleagues in composition have been delighted to learn more about the kind of writing that goes on in our classrooms.

Our Role as Scholars

Research in writing and research in our own disciplines share some significant similarities. After all, in disciplinary research, few of us expect much more than incremental progress from one paper to the next. We accept the fact that most new ideas come from altering old ones only slightly, or from combining old ideas in new ways. Only rarely will we make radically new discoveries in our disciplines, but knowing this doesn't detract from the value of our new ideas, however minor they may be. We should apply the same standard in our investigation of writing: no one of us is likely to make a discovery with paradigm-shifting potential, yet we can all make meaningful progress by seeking answers to a number of open problems regarding writing in our fields.

What more have we to learn about writing in our disciplines? Much of the existing scholarship on writing in our disciplines is anecdotal, involving descriptions of writing activities with purported learning gains and unproven benefits. While these activities are often rich and useful ones, what's missing from such accounts is a systematic treatment of, and solid evidence for, writing's efficacy in addressing students' learning needs. Following are just a few of the crucial questions needing answers; with our technical training and familiarity with our own disciplines, we are well suited to help provide those answers.

How Well Does Writing Help Improve Student Learning in Quantitative Fields?   There is a great deal of anecdotal evidence suggesting that writing in the disciplines helps students understand disciplinary content. In fact, few articles on WAC or WID methods fail to report perceptible improvement in students' understanding of course concepts after engaging writing as a learning tool. However, it's hard to measure precisely the effect that writing-to-learn techniques have on students' mastery of quantitative concepts.

A few studies indicate that WTL has little effect on learning. For instance, while Ackerman (1993) reports the positive impact of WTL on students' learning, he indicates the difficulty of separating WTL activities from other factors that promote student learning in the sorts of classroom in which WTL exercises often appear. More recently Ochsner and Fowler (2004) make a similar argument, questioning the impact of WAC and WID programs on students' learning gains and calling for greater scrutiny in spending on WAC initiatives.

However, other, more thorough reviews are more sanguine about the benefits low-stakes writing confers on students. For instance, Bangert-Drowns, Hurley, and Wilkinson (2004) provide a thorough meta-analysis of forty-eight studies of WTL activities and find that "the mean effect of writing-to-learn interventions on content achievement was rather small but significantly greater than no effect" (pp. 42–43). Happily for us, this meta-analysis found that the positive effects of WTL activities were greater in mathematics and science courses than in the overall sample. This finding is borne out by more recent work still, like Bohannon and Bohannon (2010) and Hohenshell and Hand (2006), both of which consider the impact of low-stakes writing in the high school science classroom and find this impact to be statistically significant.

It is clear from such studies that although the presence of writing may not be the only factor affecting student learning, it is an undeniably important one. However, these studies also show that we have a lot of work to do if we're to understand precisely both the extent to which writing helps students learn in our fields and the way in which it provides that help.

How Does Writing Influence Students' Affective Engagement with Their Disciplines?   We work in disciplines heavy with objective facts and formulas. The mathematical laws and physical principles that undergird our work are (often intentionally) detached and impersonalized. Therefore, as we focus on helping our students grasp difficult disciplinary concepts, it's easy for us to overlook the affective aspects of learning. Nevertheless, elements of a student's affective domain, like confidence, engagement, self-efficacy, and focus, exert a strong influence on the student's cognitive performance in quantitative fields (Hackett & Betz, 1989; Hannula, Maijala, & Pehkonen, 2004; and Hembree, 1990).

It seems obvious that carefully crafted disciplinary activities, like those described in the previous two chapters, can help students gain confidence in their ability to understand course ideas. For instance, Hilgers, Hussey, and Stitt-Bergh (1999) describe how students grew more confident about writing in their disciplinary courses (and in future discipline-specific careers) as a result of completing writing-intensive courses in their majors. Studies like this one strongly recommend more careful consideration of the affective impact of various kinds of disciplinary writing. Nevertheless we must do much more to fully understand precisely *how* these writing exercises help students, and furthermore how we can apply these exercises to maximize their effectiveness.

How Do Writers Learn to Adopt the Writing Conventions of a Particular Discipline?   We are often so close to the writing we do that we fail to notice the ways in which the fundamental aspects of our writing affect its meaning. Notation, terminology, voice (passive or active), document structure, citation style, and the overall appearance of the text on the page all make an impression on the reader, even if that impression is subtle or subconscious. We may not be aware of these rhetorical aspects as we write; nevertheless, when our attention is called to these aspects, we nod our heads and smile as though we recognized them all along.

This isn't to say that nothing is known about disciplinary rhetoric. To the contrary, many accomplished scholars have taken on the task of describing carefully the conventions of communication in their own disciplines. For instance, Charles Bazerman considers physics and its sister sciences in *Shaping Written Knowledge: The Genre and Activity of the Experimental Article in Science* (2000) and elsewhere (1984, 1985). Deirdre McCloskey analyzes economics discourse in *The Rhetoric of Economics* (1998), and Imre Lakatos's *Proofs and Refutation* (1976) dissects the genre of the mathematical proof, laying bare its rhetorical flourishes.

However, we have much yet to learn about the how beginning writers first pick up on disciplinary conventions. In their study of professional mathematicians' research writing, Burton and Morgan (2000) admit, "This study could be a starting point for work with novice (and, indeed, experienced) researchers to develop their critical linguistic awareness—their knowledge of the forms of language that are available to them and their abilities to make effective choices among them" (p. 451). My colleagues and I have begun the work hinted at here in mathematics (Bahls, Mecklenburg-Faenger, Scott-Copses, & Warnick, 2011), but this is a meager beginning. Moreover, we've no way of knowing the extent to which our work is transferrable to other fields; it's up to someone else to perform a similar analysis in physics, economics, chemistry, accounting, and other fields.

How Does Writing Help Students Enter Into the Disciplinary Community?

One way we signal our membership in a particular community is through the language we use when communicating with our peers in that community. As students learn the styles and conventions of writing in a particular discipline, they move closer to the center of that discipline's learning community. For example, the more a student writes like a physicist, the more she becomes like a physicist.

What can we do to help students make the move into our midst? Can we identify stages through which students pass as they grow accustomed to writing in our disciplines? Can we identify appropriate ways to facilitate this development at its various stages? Answering questions like these will help us equip our students to become knowledge makers and not merely knowledge fakers, for the sooner they perceive themselves to be authentic members of an academic community, the sooner they can make authentic contributions to that community.

Our Roles as Champions

On learning that I'm a mathematician, the first thing nine out of ten people say is something like "Oh, I hate math. . . . I'm really bad at it!" On the one hand, I'm offended: Are there many other professions people feel so bold in insulting? On the other hand, I cannot fully blame the speaker, for historically mathematicians have not been the most able ambassadors for their field. Much of what we do seems incomprehensibly deep, cloaked behind thick walls of data, notation, and terminology, and to make our meaning understandable to a lay audience we must often sacrifice a good deal of accuracy and precision.

This is the case for many of the quantitative sciences: the way we write can be off-putting to the uninitiated. As Montgomery insists over and over in the opening chapter of *The Scientific Voice* (1996), scientific language is cold, impersonal, and clinical: "It is a form of speech made superheavy by modes of shorthand condensation, by substitution, redefinition, fusional reduction of terms, and by the continual adding on of new and more precision-oriented nomenclature" (p. 9). If we're to break down the walls that our language builds around us, we must become advocates for writing in our disciplines; we must become its champions. We're really fighting a war on two fronts. On one front, we may have to champion WAC principles to colleagues in our own disciplines who cannot see a place for writing in these disciplines. On another front, we may have to convince disciplinary outsiders (colleagues in other departments, administrators, and so on) that we do indeed write in our fields.

Model WAC Principles for Your Colleagues No matter how happy administrators are when student learning outcomes are met, meaningful and long-lasting institutional change does not come about in response to administrative fiats or other external pressures. Faculty members are strong-willed creatures who rarely make changes simply because they're told to. Rather, we tell ourselves that we make changes because we recognize the benefit of those particular changes. When it comes to teaching, beneficial change often follows from our acknowledging the positive aspects of our colleagues' practices and adapting those practices to our own classrooms.

You can champion writing in the disciplines and writing-to-learn simply by showing how these principles work when put into play. Invite your colleagues to your classroom, to observe a lively peer review session, or to join your students in a freewrite. Share your students' writing with them, to show them how writing can be made meaningful, even in the most content-heavy courses, even in the most quantitative disciplines. Show them how you respond to students' work using minimal marking or some other efficient technique, so that they can see how writing need not take much time away from other course-related tasks.

Writing in the disciplines will catch on if you can help your colleagues to see that it can be meaningful, manageable, and fun. Although you could try telling them that disciplinary writing is all of these things, it will be much more convincing to simply show them.

Get Involved in Your Campus's Writing Program　At many institutions, WAC manifests itself in the form of a writing-intensive program. By requiring students to complete a minimum number of courses designated as "writing intensive," faculty can ensure that writing instruction doesn't end after students' first-year composition courses. In writing-intensive courses, students are exposed to writing in their major courses of study, throughout their college careers.

Many writing-intensive programs are led by members of the faculty who serve the program on a rotating basis. (Various models for writing-intensive programs are described in Farris & Smith, 2002.) These faculty oversee many aspects of the program, from establishing guidelines for writing-intensive courses to approving proposals for these courses.

Serving on your university's writing-intensive advisory committee can give you a means of learning new ways to involve writing in disciplinary courses. Indeed, members of such committees are called on to examine the writing instruction that goes on in countless contexts across the campus. I've learned more about academic writing from my tenure on my own university's writing-intensive committee than from any other single source. Moreover, I've found new friends, in a variety of disciplines, who care as deeply as I do about writing and writing instruction. This experience has helped me to see that I'm not alone in what I do, and it has helped me to explain to my colleagues in other disciplines what "writing in math" looks like.

Advocate for WAC Beyond Your Own Campus　Many institutions were quick to embrace WAC early in the movement's history, while others have taken considerably longer to adopt WAC principles. Even if your own institution has developed a rich "culture of writing," you will find that many of your colleagues at other institutions face significant obstacles to incorporating more writing into their courses.

For instance, the administration at some institutions offers little support for faculty or curricular development and just as little recognition or reward for implementing innovative ideas in the classroom. At other institutions, your colleagues may contend with teaching loads and service commitments heavy enough to dissuade them from trying anything new. You can help these colleagues by sharing your experiences regarding writing at professional meetings and conferences. Even if you're relatively new to WAC yourself, you can still share your students' successes with writing and offer some simple tips on incorporating low-stakes exercises into day-to-day coursework.

If we are to be effective ambassadors for writing in our disciplines, we must reach across disciplinary borders, even into areas where writing is commonplace but writing in our particular disciplines is poorly understood. For example, though experts in rhetoric and composition may acknowledge that a great deal of writing goes on in the quantitative disciplines, they often have little understanding of what that writing looks like. If we don't speak up, they may also feel as though their calls for our greater involvement in WAC and WID go unanswered.

While at a conference just weeks ago I attended a session on programmatic responses to writing assessment. After hearing several scholars present their respective institutions' responses to assessment data, one audience member responded, "This is all wonderful to hear, but I have a hard time believing that faculty in engineering, physics, and mathematics will be convinced that this is all worthwhile." I replied at once, assuring her that though many of us may be new to WAC, we are as devoted as faculty in any other discipline, and we are just as earnest in our efforts to make WAC work for us. If each of us is willing to take a similar stand, we won't stand alone for long.

Several decades ago the idea of writing in the disciplines was an alien one, particularly in disciplines far removed from traditionally writing-intensive areas. Who would dream that poetry might find a place in a chemistry course, or that linear algebra students could be asked to write their own textbooks, for a course they've not even completed yet?

We've come a long way, but we've far to go yet. I hope that you will continue to explore the possibilities writing offers to you and your students. Find a few of the ideas I've shared here that appeal to you, and try them out. It may take a bit of practice, but I promise you will grow more confident and competent at using writing, and so will your students. Before long you'll be coming up with new ideas of your own. Better yet, your students will, too.

RECOMMENDED READING AND RESOURCES

The resources listed here supplement the treatment provided by this book. Many provide additional examples of exercises and activities suitable for courses in various quantitative disciplines, while others explore writing in the disciplines more generally. Several of the Internet resources, like the WAC Clearinghouse and Purdue University's Online Writing Lab, offer a wide variety of tips and techniques for writing in all disciplines. Others, like PBworks and Wiggio, give technical support for writing by providing tools for composition and collaboration online.

Computer Science

Hartman, J. D. "Writing to Learn and Communicate in a Data Structures Course." *SIGCSE Bulletin,* 1989, 21(1), 32–36.

Perelman, L. C., Paradis, J., and Barrett, E. *The Mayfield Handbook of Technical and Scientific Writing.* Palo Alto, CA: Mayfield, 1998.

Zobel, J. *Writing for Computer Science* (2nd ed.). New York: Springer-Verlag, 2004.

Economics

Hansen, W. L. "Teaching a Writing Intensive Course in Economics." *Journal of Economic Education,* 1993, 24(3), 213–218.

Henry, L. H. "Clustering: Writing (and Learning) About Economics." *College Teaching,* 1986, 34(3), 89–93.

McCloskey, D. N. *The Rhetoric of Economics* (2nd ed.). Madison: University of Wisconsin Press, 1998.

McCloskey, D. N. *Economical Writing* (2nd ed.). Prospect Heights, IL: Waveland Press, 2000.

Simpson, M. S., and Carroll, S. E. "Assignments for a Writing-intensive Economics Course." *Journal of Economic Education,* 1990, 30(4), 402–410.

Tobey, D. M. "Writing Instruction in Economics Courses: Experimentation Across Disciplines." *Journal of Northeastern Agricultural Economics Council,* 1979, 8, 159–164.

Engineering

Selfe, C., and Arbabi, F. "Writing to Learn: Engineering Student Journals." In A. Young and T. Fulwiler (eds.), *Writing Across the Disciplines: Research into Practice.* Upper Montclair, NJ: Boynton/Cook, 1986.

Silyn-Roberts, H. *Writing for Science and Engineering: Papers, Presentations, and Reports.* Oxford, UK: Butterworth-Heinemann, 2000.

Sorby, S. A., and Bulleit, W. M. *An Engineer's Guide to Technical Communication.* Upper Saddle River, NJ: Pearson Prentice Hall, 2006.

Wheeler, E., and McDonald, R. L. "Writing in Engineering Courses." *Journal of Engineering Education,* 2000, 89, 481.

Winsor, D.A. *Writing Like an Engineer: A Rhetorical Education.* Mahwah, NJ: Erlbaum, 1996.

Winsor, D. A. W*riting Power: Communication in an Engineering Center.* Albany: State University of New York Press, 2003.

Mathematics and Statistics

Beins, B. C. "Writing Assignments in Statistics Classes Encourage Students to Learn Interpretation." *Teaching of Psychology,* 1993, 20, 161–164.

Burns, M. *Writing in the Math Class: A Resource for Grades 2–8.* Sausalito, CA: Math Solutions, 1995.

Clarke, D. J., Waywood, A., and Stephens, M. "Probing the Structure of Mathematical Writing." *Journal for Research in Mathematics Education,* 1993, 31(4), 235–250.

Connolly, P., and Vilardi, T. *Writing to Learn Mathematics and Science.* New York: Teachers College Press, 1989.

Drake, R. M., and Amspaugh, L. B. "What Writing Reveals in Mathematics." *Focus on Learning Problems in Mathematics,* 1994, 16(3), 43–50.

Fennema, E., and Leder, G. C. (eds.). *Mathematics and Gender.* New York: Teachers College Press, 1990.

Gerver, R. K. *Writing Math Research Papers: A Guide for Students and Instructors.* Emeryville, CA: Key Curriculum Press, 2007.

Gillman, L. *Writing Mathematics Well: A Manual for Authors.* Washington, DC: Mathematical Association of America, 1987.

Johnson, T. M., and others. "Students' Thinking and Writing in the Context of Probability." *Written Communication,* 1998, 15(2), 203–229.

Knuth, D., Larrabee, T., and Roberts, P. M. *Mathematical Writing.* Washington, DC: Mathematical Association of America, 1989.

Krantz, S. G. *A Primer of Mathematical Writing: Being a Disquisition on Having Your Ideas Recorded.* Providence, RI: American Mathematical Society, 1997.

Russek, B. "Writing to Learn Mathematics." *Writing Across the Curriculum,* 1998, 9, 36–45.

Sterrett, A. (ed.). *Using Writing to Teach Mathematics.* Washington, DC: Mathematical Association of America, 1990.

Physics

Hein, T. L. "Using Writing to Confront Student Misconceptions in Physics." *European Journal of Physics*, 1999, 20(3), 137–142.

Mullin, W. J. "Writing in Physics." *Physics Teacher*, 1989, 27(5), 342–347.

Richmond, P. E. "Writing About Physics." *Physics Education*, 1980, 15(6), 361–363.

Shield, M., and Galbraith, P. "The Analysis of Student Expository Writing in Mathematics." *Educational Studies in Mathematics*, 1998, 36(1), 29–52.

General Quantitative Sciences

Alley, M. *The Craft of Scientific Writing* (3rd ed.). New York: Springer Science+Business Media, 1996.

Chinn, P.W.U., and Hilgers, T. L. "From Corrector to Collaborator: The Range of Instructor Roles in Writing-Based Natural and Applied Science Classes." *Journal of Research in Science Teaching*, 2000, 37, 3–25.

Halliday, M.A.K., and Martin, J. R. *Writing Science: Literary and Discursive Power.* Pittsburgh: University of Pittsburgh Press, 1993.

Higham, N. J. *Handbook of Writing for the Mathematical Sciences.* Philadelphia: Society for Industrial and Applied Mathematics, 1993.

Latour, B. *Science in Action: How to Follow Scientists and Engineers Through Society.* Cambridge, MA: Harvard University Press, 1987.

Latour, B., and Woolgar, S. *Laboratory Life: The Social Construction of Scientific Facts.* Beverly Hills, CA: Sage, 1979.

Locke, D. M. *Science as Writing.* New Haven: Yale University Press, 1992.

O'Connor, M. *Writing Successfully in Science.* London and New York: E & FN Spon, 1991.

Parker, A., and Mattison, M. "By the Numbers." *WAC Journal*, 2010, 21.

Parker, J. K. *Teaching Tech-Savvy Kids: Bringing Digital Media into the Classroom, Grades 5–12.* Thousand Oaks, CA: Corwin, 2010.

Peat, J., Elliott, E., Baur, L., and Keena, V. *Scientific Writing: Easy When You Know How.* London: BMJ Books, 2002.

Pera, M., and Shea, W. (eds). *Persuading Science: The Art of Scientific Rhetoric.* Canton, MA: Science History Publishers, 1991.

Perelman, L. C., Paradis, J., and Barrett, E. *The Mayfield Handbook of Technical and Scientific Writing.* Palo Alto, CA: Mayfield, 1998.

Porter, M. K., and Masingila, J. O. "Examining the Effects of Writing on Conceptual and Procedural Knowledge in Calculus." *Educational Studies in Mathematics*, 2000, 42(2), 165–177.

Reisch, C. "Teaching Exchange: Introduction to Math Autobiography and Course Reflection Assignments. *Academic Writing.* March 2000. [http://wac.colostate.edu/aw/teaching/reisch2000/index.htm]. Retrieved September 2010.

Rivard, L. P., and Straw, S. B. "The Effect of Talk and Writing on Learning Science: An Exploratory Study." *Science Education*, 2000, 84, 566–593.

Tierney, B., and Dorroh, J. *How to . . . Write to Learn Science* (2nd ed.). Arlington, VA: NSTA Press, 2004.

General Writing

Bean, J. C. *Engaging Ideas: The Professor's Guide to Integrating Writing, Critical Thinking, and Active Learning in the Classroom.* San Francisco: Jossey-Bass, 1996.

Belanoff, P., Elbow, P., and Fontaine, S. L. (eds.). *Nothing Begins with N: New Investigations of Freewriting.* Carbondale: Southern Illinois University Press, 1991.

Connors, R. J. *Composition-Rhetoric: Backgrounds, Theory, and Pedagogy.* Pittsburgh: University of Pittsburgh Press, 1997.

Cooney, T. J., and Hirsch, C. R. (eds). *Writing to Learn Mathematics and Science.* New York: Teachers College Press, 1989.

Countryman, J. *Writing to Learn Mathematics: Strategies That Work, K–12.* Portsmouth, NH: Heinemann, 1992.

Elbow, P. *Writing Without Teachers.* New York: Oxford University Press, 1973.

Emig, J. "Writing as a Mode of Learning." *College Composition and Communication*, 1977, 28, 122–128.

Fulwiler, T. *Teaching with Writing.* Upper Montclair, NJ: Boynton/Cook, 1987.

Gottschalk, K., and Hjortshoj, K. *The Elements of Teaching Writing: A Resource for Instructors in All Disciplines.* Boston: Bedford/St. Martin's, 2004.

Leist, S. M. *Writing to Teach; Writing to Learn in Higher Education.* Lanham, MD: University Press of America, 2006.

Lindemann, E., and Tate, G. (eds). *An Introduction to Composition Studies.* New York: Oxford University Press, 1991.

Linte, C. A. "Communicating Your Research in Lay Language [Student's Corner]." *Engineering in Medicine and Biology*, 2009, 28(3), 5–7.

Peterson, A. *The Writer's Workout Book: 113 Stretches Toward Better Prose.* Berkeley, CA: Nation Writing Project, 1996.

WAC Clearinghouse, http://wac.colostate.edu.

Writing Across the Curriculum

Anson, C. M., Schweibert, J. E., and Willamson, M. M. *Writing Across the Curriculum: An Annotated Bibliography.* Westport, CT: Greenwood, 1993.

Bazerman, C., Little, J., Bethel, L., Chavkin, T., Fouquette, D., and Garufis, J. *Reference Guide to Writing Across the Curriculum*, 2005. Parlor Press and WAC Clearinghouse. [http://wac.colostate.edu/books/bazerman_wac/]. Retrieved December 2010.

Bazerman, C., and Russell, D. R. (eds). *Landmark Essays on Writing Across the Curriculum.* Davis, CA: Hermagoras, 1994.

Brereton, J.C. (ed.). *The Origin of Composition Studies in the American College, 1875–1925: A Documentary History*. Pittsburgh: University of Pittsburgh Press, 1995.

Britton, J. *Language and Learning*. Portsmouth, NH: Boynton/Cook, 1970.

Fulwiler, T. "How Well Does Writing Across the Curriculum Work?" *College Composition and Communication*, 1984, 46(2), 113–125.

Herrington, A. J. "Writing to Learn: Writing Across the Disciplines." *College English*, 1981, 43, 379–387.

Maimon, E. "WAC: Past, Present and Future." In C. W. Griffin (ed.), *Teaching Writing in All Disciplines*. San Francisco: Jossey-Bass, 1982.

McCarthy, L. P. "A Stranger in Strange Lands: A College Student Writing Across the Curriculum." *Research in the Teaching of English*, 1987, 21, 233–365.

McLeod, S. (ed.). *Strengthening Programs for Writing Across the Curriculum*. San Francisco: Jossey-Bass, 1988.

McLeod, S., Miraglia, E., Soven, M., and Thaiss, C. (eds.). *WAC for the New Millennium: Strategies for Continuing Writing-Across-the-Curriculum Programs*. Urbana, IL: National Council of Teachers of English, 2001.

McLeod, S., and Soven, M. (eds.). *Writing Across the Curriculum: A Guide to Developing New Programs*. Newbury Park, CA: Sage, 1992.

Monroe, J. (ed.). *Writing and Revising in the Disciplines*. Ithaca, NY: Cornell University Press, 2002.

Montgomery, S. *The Scientific Voice*. New York: Guilford, 1996.

Parker, R. P., and Goodkin, V. *The Consequences of Writing: Enhancing Learning in the Disciplines*. Upper Montclair, NJ: Boynton/Cook, 1987.

Payne, L. "Using a Wiki to Support Sustainability Literacy." *Innovations in Teaching and Learning in Information and Computer Science*, 2009, 8(1). [http://www.ics.heacademy.ac.uk/italics/vol8iss1.htm]. Retrieved March 2011.

Russell, D. R. *Writing in the Academic Disciplines, 1870–1990: A Curricular History*. Carbondale: Southern Illinois University Press, 1991.

Vygotsky, L. S. *Thought and Language* (E. Hanfmann and G. Vakar, trans.). Cambridge, MA: MIT Press, 1962.

"Why Johnny Can't Write." *Newsweek*, December 8, 1975, pp. 58–65.

Young, A., and Fulwiler, T. *Writing Across the Disciplines: Research into Practice*. Upper Montclair, NJ: Boynton/Cook, 1986.

Internet Resources

Bahls, P. *Change of Basis*. [http://changeofbasis.blogspot.com]. March 2011.

The Bill & Melinda Gates Foundation. [http://www.gatesfoundation.org]. July 2011.

George Mason University. *Writing Across the Curriculum*. [http://wac.gmu.edu]. March 2011.

Google Sites. [http://sites.google.com]. April 2011.

International WAC Network. [http://wac.colostate.edu/network/]. March 2011.

North Carolina State University Department of Mathematics. *Department of Mathematics Writing and Speaking Outcomes.* [http://www.chass.ncsu.edu/CWSP/docs/Math_out.pdf]. December 2010.

PBworks: Online Collaboration. [http://pbworks.com]. April 2011.

Purdue University English Department. *The Purdue Online Writing Lab (OWL).* [http://owl.english.purdue.edu/]. March 2011.

University of North Carolina Asheville. "Class Schedule Description, Social Justice and Math." [http://www2.unca.edu/registrar/classes/schedules/viewer.asp?semester=201110&course=MATH273001&crn=10727&title=ST:DI:Social%20Justice%20and%20Math]. http://www2.unca.edu/registrar/classes/schedules]. December 2010.

WAC Clearinghouse. [http://wac.colostate.edu]. September 2011.

Wiggio. [http://wiggio.com]. April 2011.

Wikipedia. [http://wikipedia.org]. January 2011.

REFERENCES

Ackerman, J. "The Promise of Writing to Learn." *Written Communication*, 1993, 10, 334–370.

Alber, M. "Creative Writing in Chemistry." *Journal of Chemistry Education*, 2001, 78(4), 478–480.

Allen, D., and Tanner, K. "Rubrics: Tools for Making Learning Goals and Evaluation Criteria Explicit for Both Teachers and Learners." *CBE-Life Sciences Education*, 2006, 5, 197–206.

Alley, M. *The Craft of Scientific Writing* (3rd ed.). New York: Springer Science+Business Media, 1996.

American Association for the Advancement of Science. "Benchmarks for Science Literacy," 1993. [http://www.project2061.org/tools/benchol/bolintro.htm]. Retrieved November 2010.

Angelo, T. A., and Cross, K .P. *Classroom Assessment Techniques* (2nd ed.). San Francisco: Jossey-Bass, 1993.

Anson, C. M. (ed.). *The WAC Casebook*. New York and Oxford: Oxford University Press, 2002.

Anson, C. M. "Assessment in Action: A Möbius Tale." In M. Hundleby and J. Allen (eds.), *Assessment in Technical and Professional Communication*. Amityville, NY: Baywood, 2009.

Anson, C. M., and Beach, R. *Journals in the Classroom: Writing to Learn*. Norwood, MA: Christopher-Gordon, 1995.

Anson, C. M., and Dannels, D. "Profiling Programs: Formative Uses of Departmental Consultations in the Assessment of Communication Across the Curriculum." *Across the Disciplines*, 2009, 6. [http://wac.colostate.edu/atd/assessment/anson_dannels.cfm]. Retrieved March 2011.

Arter, J., and McTighe, J. *Scoring Rubrics in the Classroom: Using Performance Criteria for Assessing and Improving Student Performance*. Thousand Oaks, CA: Corwin, 2001.

Audet, R. H., Hickman, P., and Dobrynina, G. "Learning Logs: A Classroom Practice for Enhancing Scientific Sense Making." *Journal of Research in Science Teaching*, 1996, 33, 205–222.

Axelrod, R. B., and Cooper, C. R. *Concise Guide to Writing* (6th ed.). Boston: Bedford/St. Martin's, 2010.

Bahls, P. "Math and Metaphor: Using Poetry to Teach College Mathematics." *WAC Journal*, 2009, 20, 75–90.

Bahls, P. "Wha . . . ? A new *post*!? (Complete with interrobang. . .)." [http://changeofbasis.blogspot.com/2010/03/wha-new-post-complete-with-interrobang.html]. Retrieved April 2011.

Bahls, P., Mecklenburg-Faenger, A., Scott-Copses, M., and Warnick, C. "Proofs and Persuasion: A Cross-Disciplinary Analysis of Math Students' Writing." *Across the Disciplines*, 2011, 8(1). [http://wac.colostate.edu/atd/articles/bahlsetal2011/index.cfm]. Retrieved July 2011.

Baker, J. H. "The Learning Log." *Journal of Information Systems Education*, 2003, 14(1), 11–14.

Bangert-Drowns, R. L., Hurley, M. M., and Wilkinson, B. "The Effects of School-Based Writing-to-Learn Interventions on Academic Achievement: A Meta-Analysis." *Review of Educational Research*, 2004, 74(1), 29–58.

Bazerman, C. "The Writing of Scientific Non-Fiction: Contexts, Choices and Constraints." *Pre/Text*, 1984, 5, 39–74.

Bazerman, C. "Physicists Reading Physics: Schema-Laden Purposes and Purpose-Laden Schema." *Written Communication*, 1985, 2, 3–23.

Bazerman, C. *Shaping Written Knowledge: The Genre and Activity of the Experimental Article in Science*. WAC Clearinghouse Landmark Publications in Writing Studies, 2000. [http://wac.colostate.edu/books/bazerman_shaping/]. Retrieved March 2011.

Bazerman, C., Little, J., Bethel, L., Chavkin, T., Fouquette, D., and Garufis, J. *Reference Guide to Writing Across the Curriculum*, 2005. Parlor Press and WAC Clearinghouse. [http://wac.colostate.edu/books/bazerman_wac/]. Retrieved December 2010.

Beach, R., and Friedrich, T. "Response to Writing." In C. A. MacArthur, S. Graham, and J. Fitzgerald (eds.), *Handbook of Writing Research*. New York: Guilford, 2006.

Beach, R., Anson, C. M., Kastman-Breuch, L.-A., and Swiss, T. *Teaching Writing Using Blogs, Wikis, and Other Digital Tools*. Norwood, MA: Christopher-Gordon, 2009.

Bean, J. *Engaging Ideas: The Professor's Guide to Integrating Writing, Critical Thinking, and Active Learning in the Classroom*. San Francisco: Jossey-Bass, 1996.

Belanoff, P., Elbow, P., and Fontaine, S. L. (eds.). *Nothing Begins with N: New Investigations of Freewriting*. Carbondale: Southern Illinois University Press, 1991.

Bohannon, C., and Bohannon, J. "Penning a Science Narrative: Assessing WAC as Curriculum Support." Paper presented at the Tenth Biannual International Writing Across the Curriculum Conference, Bloomington, IN, May 2010.

Bossavit, L., and Gaillot, E. "Lightning Writing Workshop Exchange Ideas on Improving Writing Skills." In *Extreme Programming and Agile Processes in Software Engineering*. Lecture Notes in Computer Science, no. 3556. New York: Springer-Verlag, 2005.

Braga, J., and Kantz, M. R., "Writing Haiku as an Activity in a Fundamentals of Chemistry Class." *Journal of Chemistry Education*, 2010, 87(10), Letter.

Brannon, L., and others. *Thinking Out Loud on Paper: The Student Daybook as a Tool for Fostering Learning.* Portsmouth, NH: Heinemann, 2008.

Brereton, J. C. (ed.). *The Origin of Composition Studies in the American College, 1875–1925: A Documentary History.* Pittsburgh: University of Pittsburgh Press, 1995.

Brewer, S. M., and Jozefowicz, J. J. "Making Economics Principles Personal: Student Journals and Reflection Papers." *Journal of Economic Education,* 2007, 37(2), 202–216.

Britton, J. *Language and Learning.* Portsmouth, NH: Boynton/Cook, 1970.

Brown, G. "Writing Mathematical Dialogues." *American Mathematical Monthly,* 1986, 93(4), 296–298.

Burton, L., and Morgan, C. "Mathematicians Writing." *Journal for Research in Mathematics Education,* 2000, 31(4), 429–453.

Cahnmann, M. "The Craft, Practice, and Possibility of Poetry in Educational Research." *Educational Researcher,* 2003, 32(3), 29–36.

Campbell, O. J. "The Failure of Freshman English." *English Journal,* 1939, 28(3), 177–185.

Carter, M. "Ways Knowing, Doing, and Writing in the Disciplines." *College Composition and Communication,* 2007, 58(3), 385–418.

Carter, M., Anson, C. M., and Miller, C. R. "Assessing Technical Writing in Institutional Contexts: Using Outcome-Based Assessment for Programmatic Thinking." *Technical Communication Quarterly,* 2003, 12(1), 101–114.

Carter, M., Ferzli, M., and Wiebe, E. N. "Writing to Learn by Learning to Write in the Disciplines." *Journal of Business and Technical Communication,* 2007, 21(3), 278–302.

Clark, I. L. (ed.). *Concepts in Composition: Theory and Practice in the Teaching of Writing.* Mahwah, NJ: Lawrence Erlbaum, 2003.

Coghill, D. E., Orzolek, B., Prichard, F., and Westmoreland, L. "Research Writing: The Whole in the Middle." Paper presented at the Tenth International Writing Across the Curriculum Conference, Bloomington, IN, May 2010.

Connor-Greene, P. A., and others (eds). *Teaching and Learning Creatively: Inspirations and Reflections.* West Lafayette, IN: Parlor Press, 2006.

Cooney, T. J., and Hirsch, C. R. (eds.). *Writing to Learn Mathematics and Science.* New York: Teachers College Press, 1989.

Countryman, J. *Writing to Learn Mathematics: Strategies That Work, K–12.* Portsmouth, NH: Heinemann, 1992.

Cowan, G., and Cowan, E. *Writing.* New York: Wiley, 1980.

Crannell, A., LaRose, G., Ratliff, T., and Rykken, E. *Writing Projects for Mathematics Courses: Crushed Clowns, Cars, and Coffee to Go.* Washington, DC: Mathematical Association of America, 2004.

Deremer, D. "Improving the Learning Environment in CS I: Experiences with Communication Strategies." *ACM SIGCSE Bulletin,* 1993, 25(3).

Downs, D., and Wardle, E. "Teaching About Writing, Righting Misconceptions: (Re) envisioning 'First-Year Composition' as 'Introduction to Writing Studies.'" *College Composition and Communication,* 2007, 58(4), 552–584.

Dunn, P. A. *Talking, Sketching, Moving: Multiple Literacies in the Teaching of Writing.* Upper Montclair, NJ: Boynton/Cook, 2001.

Elbow, P. *Writing Without Teachers.* New York: Oxford University Press, 1973.

Elbow, P. *Embracing Contraries: Explorations in Learning and Teaching.* New York: Oxford University Press, 1986.

Elbow, P. *Writing with Power: Techniques for Mastering the Writing Process* (2nd ed.). New York: Oxford University Press, 1998.

Emig, J. *The Composing Processes of Twelfth Graders.* Urbana, IL: National Council of Teachers of English, 1971.

Emmerich, P. J. "Written Composition Outside the English Class." *Journal of English Teaching Techniques,* 1968, 1(4), 5–8.

Fahnestock, J. *Rhetorical Figures in Science.* New York: Oxford University Press, 1999.

Farris, C., and Smith, R. "Writing Intensive Courses: Tools for Curricular Change." In S. MacLeod and M. Soven (eds.), *Writing Across the Curriculum: A Guide to Developing Programs.* Newbury Park, CA: Sage, 2002.

Findley, T. "The Fever Dream: A Personal Narrative Exercise." [http://www.edutopia.org/blog/write-compose-personal-narrative-fever-dream]. Retrieved March 2011.

Fink, L. D. *Creating Significant Learning Experiences: An Integrated Approach to Designing College Courses.* San Francisco: Jossey-Bass, 2003.

Gardner, S., and Fulwiler, T. (eds.). *The Journal Book for Teachers in Technical and Professional Programs.* Westport, CT: Boynton, 1998.

Gerver, R. K. *Writing Math Research Papers: A Guide for Students and Instructors.* Emeryville, CA: Key Curriculum, 2007.

Glesne, C. E. "That Rare Feeling: Re-presenting Research Through Poetic Transcription." *Qualitative Inquiry,* 1997, 3, 202–221.

Goma, O. D. "Creative Writing in Economics." *College Teaching,* 2001, 49(4), 149–152.

Gopen, G., and Smith, D. "What's an Assignment Like You Doing in a Course Like This? Writing to Learn Mathematics." *College Mathematics Journal,* 1990, 21, 2–19.

Gottschalk, K., and Hjortshoj, K. *The Elements of Teaching Writing: A Resource for Instructors in All Disciplines.* Boston: Bedford/St. Martin's, 2004.

Gragson, D. E., and Hagen, J. P. "Developing Technical Writing Skill in the Physical Chemistry Laboratory: A Progressive Approach Employing Peer Review." *Journal of Chemical Education,* 2010, 87 (1), 62–65.

Green, D. H. "Student-Generated Exams: Testing and Learning." *Journal of Marketing Education,* 1997, 19(2), 45–53.

Hackett, G., and Betz, N. E. "An Exploration of the Mathematics Self-Efficacy/Mathematics Performance Correspondence." *Journal of Research in Mathematics Education,* 1989, 20(3), 261–273.

Hand, B., and Prain, V. "Teachers Implementing Writing-to-Learn Strategies in Junior Secondary Science: A Case Study." *Science Education,* 2002, 86, 737–755.

Hand, B., Wallace, C., and Yang, E. "Using the Science Writing Heuristic to Enhance Learning Outcomes from Laboratory Activities in Seventh Grade Science: Quantitative and Qualitative Aspects." *International Journal of Science Education*, 2000, 26(2), 131–149.

Hannula, M. S., Maijala, H., and Pehkonen, E. "Development of Understanding and Self Confidence in Mathematics." *Proceedings of the Twenty-Eighth International Group for the Psychology of Mathematics Education*, Bergen, Norway, 2004.

Haslam, M., and Pelayo, R. "Summer Intensive Math Learning Logs, Keaholoa Summer Intensive Math Workshop, University of Hawai'i-Hilo." [http://www2.hawaii.edu/~robertop/SI/LL.html]. Retrieved December 2010.

Haswell, R. H. "Minimal Marking." *College English*, 1983, 45, 600–604.

Hembree, R. "The Nature, Effects, and Relief of Mathematics Anxiety." *Journal for Research in Mathematics Education*, 1990, 21(1), 33–46.

Hilgers, T. L., Hussey, E. L., and Stitt-Bergh, M. "'As You're Writing, You Have These Epiphanies': What College Students Say About Writing and Learning in Their Majors." *Written Communication*, 1999, 16(3), 317–353.

Hohenshell, L. M., and Hand, B. "Writing-to-Learn Strategies in Secondary School Cell Biology: A Mixed Method Study." *International Journal of Science Education*, 2006, 28(2–3), 261–289.

Huba, M. E., and Freed, J. E. *Learner-Centered Assessment on College Campuses: Shifting the Focus from Teaching to Learning.* Boston: Allyn & Bacon, 2000.

Jablonski, J., and Weiser, I. "Raising the Gates on Chem. 110." In C. M. Anson (ed.), *The WAC Casebook.* New York: Oxford University Press, 2002.

Kantrowitz, B. M. "What Price Technical Editing? I: Reaching a Lay Audience." *IEEE Transactions on Professional Communication*, 1985, 28(1), 13–19.

Keane, A., and Gibson, I. S. "Communication Trends in Engineering Firms: Implications for Undergraduate Engineering Courses." *International Journal of Engineering Education*, 1999, 15(2), 115–121.

Kent, T. (ed.). *Post-Process Theory: Beyond the Writing-Process Paradigm.* Carbondale: Southern Illinois University Press, 1999.

Kiefer, K., and Leff, A. "Client-Based Writing About Science: Immersing Science Students in Real Writing Contexts." *Across the Disciplines*, 2008, 5.

King, B. "Using Writing in the Mathematics Class: Theory and Practice." *New Directions for Teaching and Learning*, 1982, 12, 39–44.

Krantz, S. G. *A Primer of Mathematical Writing: Being a Disquisition on Having Your Ideas Recorded.* Providence, RI: American Mathematical Society, 1997.

Kuhn, T. *The Structure of Scientific Revolutions.* Chicago: University of Chicago Press, 1962.

Lakatos, I. *Proofs and Refutations.* Cambridge, UK: University of Cambridge Press, 1976.

Lehman, A. "Technical Writing: English for a Lay Audience." *Teaching English in the Two-Year College*, 1979, 6(1), 67–70.

Leist, S. M. *Writing to Teach; Writing to Learn in Higher Education.* Lanham, MD: University Press of America, 2006.

Lindemann, E. *A Rhetoric for Writing Teachers.* New York: Oxford University Press, 1995.

Linte, C. A. "Communicating Your Research in Lay Language [Student's Corner]." *Engineering in Medicine and Biology,* 2009, 28(3), 5–7.

Luft, J. A. "Rubrics: Design and Use in Science Teacher Education." *Journal of Science Teacher Education,* 1999, 10, 107–121.

Lynd-Balta, E. "Using Literature and Innovative Assessments to Ignite Interest and Cultivate Critical Thinking Skills in an Undergraduate Neuroscience Course." *CBE-Life Sciences Education,* 2006, 5, 167–174.

Maimon, E. "WAC: Past, Present and Future." In C. W. Griffin (ed.), *Teaching Writing in All Disciplines.* San Francisco: Jossey-Bass, 1982.

McCloskey, D. N. *Economical Writing* (2nd ed.). Prospect Heights, IL: Waveland, 2000.

McDermott, R., Eccleston, G., and Brindley, G. "More Than a Good Story: Can You Really Teach Programming Through Storytelling?" *Innovations in Teaching and Learning in Information and Computer Science,* 2008, 7(1). [http://www.ics.heacademy.ac.uk/italics/vol7iss1.htm]. Retrieved March 2011.

McIntosh, M. E., and Draper, R. J. "Using Learning Logs in Mathematics: Writing to Learn." *Mathematics Teacher,* 2001, 94(7), 554–557.

Meier, J., and Rishel, T. *Writing in the Teaching and Learning of Mathematics.* Washington, DC: Mathematical Association of America, 1998.

Melzer, D. "Assignments Across the Curriculum: A Survey of College Writing." *Language and Learning Across the Disciplines,* 2003, 86–110.

Montgomery, S. L. *The Scientific Voice.* New York: Guilford, 1996.

Murray, D. "Teach Writing as a Process Not Product." *Leaflet,* Fall 1972, 11–14.

Myers, J. W. W*riting to Learn Across the Curriculum.* Bloomington, IN: Phi Delta Kappa Educational Foundation, 1984.

Nilson, L. B. "Improving Student Peer Feedback." *College Teaching,* 2003, 51(1), 34–38.

O'Connor, M. *Writing Successfully in Science.* London and New York: E & FN Spon, 1991.

Ochsner, R., and Fowler, J. "Playing Devil's Advocate: Evaluating the Literature of the WAC/WID Movement." *Review of Educational Research,* 2004, 74(2), 117–140.

Olds, B. M., Dyrud, M. A., Held, J. A., and Sharp, J. E. "Writing in Engineering and Technology Courses." Frontiers in Education Conference (Twenty-Third Annual Conference), "Engineering Education: Renewing America's Technology," *Proceedings,* 1993, 618–623.

Ostheimer, M. W., Mylrea, K. C., and Lonsdale, E. M. "An Integrated Course in Fundamental Engineering and English Composition Using Interactive and Process Learning Methodologies." *IEEE Transactions on Education,* 1994, 37(2), 189–193.

Parke, C. S., "Reasoning and Communicating in the Language of Statistics." *Journal of Statistics Education,* 2008, 16(1). [http://www.amstat.org/publications/jse/v16n1/parke.html]. Retrieved March 2011.

Parker, J. K. *Teaching Tech-Savvy Kids: Bringing Digital Media into the Classroom, Grades 5-10.* Thousand Oaks, CA: Corwin, 2010.

Payne, L. "Using a Wiki to Support Sustainability Literacy." *Innovations in Teaching and Learning in Information and Computer Science*, 2009, 8(1). [http://www.ics.heacademy.ac.uk/italics/vol8iss1.htm]. Retrieved March 2011.

Peterson, A. *The Writer's Workout Book: 113 Stretches Toward Better Prose*. Berkeley, CA: Nation Writing Project, 1996.

Phillips, E., and Crespo, S. "Developing Written Communication in Mathematics Through Math Penpal Letters." *For the Learning of Mathematics*, 1996, 16(1), 15–22.

Piaget, J. *The Language and Thought of the Child*. (M. Gabain and R. Gabain, trans.) London and New York: Routledge Classics, 2002.

Richardson, L. "The Consequences of Poetic Representation: Writing the Other, Writing the Self." In C. Ellis and M.G. Flaherty (eds.), *Investigating Subjectivity: Research on Lived Experience*. Newbury Park, CA: Sage, 1992.

Richardson, L. "Writing: A Method of Inquiry." In N. K. Denzin and Y. S. Lincoln (eds.), *Handbook of Qualitative Research* (2nd ed.). Newbury Park, CA: Sage, 2000.

Russell, D. R. "American Origins of the Writing-Across-the-Curriculum Movement." In C. Bazerman and D. Russell (eds.), *Landmark Essays in Writing Across the Curriculum*. Davis, CA: Hermagoras Press, 1994.

Russell, D. R. *Writing in the Academic Disciplines, 1870–1990: A Curricular History*. Carbondale: Southern Illinois University Press, 1991.

Samuels, F. "Using Poetry to Teach Sociology." *Teaching Sociology*, 1987, 15, 55–60.

Schriver, K. A. "Revising for Readers: Audience Awareness in the Writing Classroom." In A. M. Penrose and B. M. Sitko (eds.), *Hearing Ourselves Think: Cognitive Research in the College Writing Classroom*. New York: Oxford University Press, 1993.

Sgoutas-Emch, S. A., and Johnson, C. J. "Is Journal Writing an Effective Method of Reducing Anxiety Towards Statistics?" *Journal of Instructional Psychology*, 1998, 25, 49–57.

Sharp, J. E., Harb, J. N., and Terry, R. E. "Combining Kolb Learning Styles and Writing to Learn in Engineering Classes." *Journal of Engineering Education*, 1997, 86(2), 93–101.

Smart, R., Hudd, S., Delohery, A., Pritchett, G., and Hoffman, M. "'Naked Language': Writing to Advance the Disciplines, a New Rhetoric." Panel presentation at the Tenth International Writing Across the Curriculum Conference, Bloomington, IN, May 2010.

Smith, H. M., Broughton, A., and Copley, J. "Evaluating the Written Work of Others: One Way Economics Students Can Learn to Write." *Journal of Economic Education*, 2006, 36(1), 43–58.

Smith, S., "The Genre of the End Comment: Conventions in Teacher Responses to Student Writing." *College Composition and Communication*, 1997, 48(2), 249–268.

Sommers, N. "Responding to Student Writing." *College Composition and Communication*, 1982, 33(2), 148–156.

Sorby, S. A., and Bulleit, W. M. *An Engineer's Guide to Technical Communication*. Upper Saddle River, NJ: Pearson Prentice Hall, 2006.

Timbur, J. *The Call to Write* (brief 5th ed.). Boston: Wadsworth, 2010.

Topping, K. "Peer Assessment Between Students in Colleges and Universities." *Review of Educational Research,* 1998, 68, 249–276.

van Ryswyk, H. V. "Writing-Intensive Multimedia Projects in the Instrumental Methods Course." *Journal of Chemistry Education,* 2005, 81, 70–72.

Vygotsky, L. S. *Thought and Language.* (E. Hanfmann and G. Vakar, trans.) Cambridge, MA: MIT Press, 1962.

WAC Clearinghouse. [http://wac.colostate.edu/]. Retrieved January 2011.

Zimmerman, B J., and Kitsantas, A. "Acquiring Writing Revision and Self-Regulatory Skill Through Observation and Emulation." *Journal of Educational Psychology,* 2002, 94(4), 660–668.

Zobel, J. *Writing for Computer Science* (2nd ed.). New York: Springer-Verlag, 2004.

INDEX

Griffin, C. W., 18
Guiding conceptual development: learning logs for, 99–101; student-authored exam questions, 101–105. *See also* Comprehension

H

Hackett, G., 89, 120, 140
Hagen, J. P., 64
Hand, B., 139
Hannula, M. S., 89, 120, 140
Harb, J. N., 90
Haslam, M., 100
Haswell, R. H., 56
Haugh, J., 123–125
Held, J. A., 79
Hembree, R., 89, 120, 140
Hickman, P., 90, 100
Hilgers, T. L., 140
Hjortshoj, K., xv, 38
Hoffman, M., 66–67
Hohenshell, L. M., 139
Homework committees, xvi, 71–73
Huba, M. E., 60
Hudd, S., 66
Hurley, M. M., 139
Hussey, E. L., 140

I

In-class peer reviews, 68–71
Innovations in Teaching and Learning in Information and Computer Science, 131
International Journal of Engineering Education, 131
International WAC Network, 132
International Writing Across the Curriculum Conference, 132
Internet resources, 132, 145, 149–150

J

Jablonski, J., 33
James, C., 108–109
Johnson, C. J., 90
Johnston, S., 34
Journal of Chemistry Education, 131
Journal of College Science Teaching, 131
Journal of Engineering Education, 131
Journal of Information Systems Education, 131

Journal of Mathematics Teacher Education, 131
Journal of Research in Mathematics Education, 131
Journal of Research in Science Teaching, 131
Journal of Statistics Education, 132
Journaling: faculty, 134–135; student, 88–90
Jozefowicz, J. J., 90

K

Kalauli, A., 101
Kantrowitz, B. M., 108
Kantz, M. R., 120, 122
Kaplan, S., 114–117
Kastman-Breuch, L.-A., 84
Keane, A., 108
Keifer, K., 117
Kent, T., 22
King, B., 79
Krantz, S. G., 50
Kuhn, T., 15

L

Lakatos, I., 23, 141
Language and Learning (Britton), 18
LaQuerre, K., 124–125
LaRose, G., xvii
LaTex, 35, 127–128
Learning: art of assessment and response, 47–49; bottom-up, 100, 101; describing outcomes for, 37–38; engaging writing strategies for, xv; how to use assignments, 129, 132–133; improving with writing in disciplines, 139–140. *See also* Comprehension
Learning logs: guiding conceptual development with, 99–101; reviewing and responding to, xv–xvi
Leff, A., 117
Lehman, A., 108
Lindemann, E. A., 55
Linhart, J. M., 83
Linte, C. A., 108
Lonsdale, E. M., 79
Looping, 78–79
Low-stakes writing: benefits of, 75–76; daybooks, 91–92; dialogue exercises, xvii, 10, 84–86; doubting and believing game, 80–82; effectiveness of, 139–140; estimation essays,

11, 86–88; evolution of, 5; examples of, 10–11; freewriting, 77–78; journaling, 88–90; readings and resources for, 96; three-minute themes, 82–84; time capsule letters, 92–94. *See also* Freewriting

Lucas Letter, A, 108

Luft, J. A., 60

Lynd-Balta, E., 60

M

Maijala, H., 89, 120, 140

Maimon, E., 5, 6, 18

Mapping courses, 27, 28

Mathematics: calculus writing exercises, xii–xiii, 82, 124; clustering for, 26–27; completeness of, 52; dialogue exercises in, 85; doubting and believing exercise in, 82; proposals for, 40; readings and resources for, 19, 146; Watchword exercise for, 98–99; writing in, xii–xiv, 109; writing proofs, xvii, 22–24, 34–35, 52, 98–99

McCloskey, D. N., 50, 141

McDermott, R., 127

McIntosh, M. E., 100

McTighe, J., 58, 60

Mecklenburg-Faenger, A., 141

Meier, J., xviii

Melzer, D., 100

Microgenres, 11, 83–84

Miller, C. R., 45

Minimal marking, 56

Montgomery, S. L., 16, 142

Morgan, C., 141

Murray, D., 24

Mylrea, K. C., 79

N

National Council of Teachers of English, 132

Networking with writing professionals, 138

Nilson, L. B., 64, 67, 69

North Carolina State University, 44–45

O

O'Connor, M., 50

Olds, B. M., 79

Online peer reviews, 73–74

Online Writing Lab, 132

Organizing writing: about, 24; annotated bibliographies for, 30–31; reverse outlines, 32; using outlines, 29–30

Origin of Composition Studies in the American College, The (Brereton), 18

Orzolek, B., 30, 31

Oschner, R., 139

Ostheimer, M. W., 79

Outlines, 29–30, 32

Overcoming resistance: faculty, 12–14; to peer review, 63–64; to review and revision process, 33; student, 14, 17–18

P

Paragraphs, 51–52

Parke, C. S., 64

Parker, J. K., 84

Payne, L., 117

Peer reviews, 63–74; benefits of, 63–64; criteria for, 70–71; evaluating grant proposals, 115–116; initiating student writing, xv; online, 73–74; preparing students for, 64–68; questions helpful in, 57–58; reviewing professional writing, 66–67; structuring in-class, 68–71; for student-authored exam questions, 102, 103; using homework committees for, xvi, 71–73; via online Wiki, 118

Pehkonen, E., 89, 120, 140

Pelayo, R., 100–101

Periodicals, 131–132

Peterson, A., 28–29, 38, 77

Phillips, E., 109

Physics: dialogue exercises in, 86; proposals for, 41; readings and resources for, 147; writing for lay audience in, 109

Piaget, J., 5

Poetry: assignments for, xvi, 120–123; engaging students in discipline with, 130

Posters, 10

Prewriting, 25–29; about, 24; clustering strategies, 26–27; freewriting as part of, 26; organizing ideas in, 29; requiring in assignments, 38–39; *See also* Freewriting

Prichard, F., 30

Pritchett, G., 66

Process: encouraging product over, 15–16; writing as, 34–35, 48

Proofreading vs. revisions, 55

Sharing: own writing, 60–61, 62–63; writing ideas with others, 135–137

Sharp, J. E., 79, 90

Smart, R., 66

Smith, D. A., 57–58

Smith, H. M., 64

Smith, R., 143

Smith, S., 55

Sommers, N., 55

Sorby, S. A., 50

Speaking, 45

Statistics: dialogue exercises in, 86; proposals for, 40; readings and resources for, 146; rubrics for, 58–59; uses of clustering for, 27

Stitt-Bergh, M., 140

Structure of Scientific Revolutions, The (Kuhn), 15

Structuring in-class peer reviews, 68–71

Structuring writing assignments, 36–42; annotated bibliographies, 30–31, 39; helping students start assignments, 38; including review and revision, 41–42; making learning outcomes clear, 37–38; proposals, 39–41; providing authentic writing assignments, 8–9; requiring prewriting, 38–39; as single step, 36–37; time required, x–xi, xv–xvi, 36

Student-authored exam questions, 101–105

Student-authored textbooks, 110–113

Students: annotated bibliographies by, 30–31, 39; creating and responding to time capsule letters, 92–94; creating exam questions, 101–105; errors in problem-solving focus, 14–16; face-to-face conferencing for, 61–63; feedback benefits for, xiv; generating assessment criteria, 53; helping start assignments, 38; learning quantitative discipline conventions, 140–141; low-stakes writing for, 75–76; participating in Great Debates, 105–106; preparing for peer reviews, 64–68; recognizing evolution of writing in course, 43; reflecting on writing process, 34–35; resistance to WAC, 14, 17–18; showing examples of revisions, 60–61; using review phase in writing, 32–33; writing peer reviews for, xv

Summative feedback, 49

Swiss, T., 84

T

Tanner, K., 60

Teachers: benefits of low-stakes writing for, 76; championing writing, 130–137, 142–144; creating assignments, 36–37; daybook reviews by, 92; documenting assignment responses, 133–135; encouraging product over process, 15–16; face-to-face student conferences with, 61–63; first attempts at teaching writing, xiii–xiv; guiding revisions, 53–63; journaling by, 134–135; learning to assess writing, 47–49; overcoming resistance to WAC, 12–14; peer review preparations by, 64–68; recognizing good writing, 49–53; responding honestly, 57–58; reviewing journals, 90; role as, 137–138; as scholar, 138–141; sharing ideas with others, 135–137; showing feedback on own writing, 60–61, 62–63; understanding tradition of disciplinary writing, 1–3; writing revision end notes, 55–56. *See also* Time requirements for teachers

Teaching Writing in All Disciplines (Griffin), 18

Technical typesetting, 127–128

Terry, R. E., 90

Textbooks: student-authored, xvii, 110–113; student-selected, 66–67

Thought and Language (Vygotsky), 5, 18

Three-minute themes, 82–84

Timbur, J., 25

Time capsule letters, 92–94

Time requirements for teachers: creating effective responses, 55–56; face-to-face conferencing requirements, 61–63; grading low-stakes writing, 94–96; required for writing activities, x–xi, xv–xvi, 36

Tutorial websites, 118–119

Twitter, 11, 83

V

Van Ryswyk, H. V., 125

Vygotsky, L., 5, 18

W

WAC. *See* Writing across curriculum

WAC Casebook, The, 33

WAC Clearinghouse, 132

WAC Journal, 6, 131

Warnick, C., 141

Watchword exercise, 98–99

Web: developing wikis and websites on, 117–119; free online design tools for, 119; Internet resources on, 145, 149–150; writing resources on, 132

Weiser, I., 33

Westmoreland, L., 30

"What's an Assignment Like You Doing in a Course Like This?" (Gopen and Smith), 57–58

Wiebe, E. N., 23

Wikis and other websites, 117–119

Wilkinson, B., 139

Writer's Workout Book, The (Peterson), 28–29, 77

Writing: about, 21–22; assuming persona for, 106–107; clearly, 51; completeness in, 50–51, 52; composition and rhetoric studies in, 4–5; continuity between courses, 43–46; developing outcomes for, 45; draft phase of, 24, 31–33, 53–54; encouraging self-reflection on, 34–35; evaluating composition of, 50, 51–52; finding resources for, xvii–xviii; Four Cs of writing, 50–53; learning discipline's conventions for, 140–141; learning to critique, 47–49; mathematical proofs, xvii, 22–24, 34–35, 52, 98–99; organizing and outlining, 24, 29–31; prewriting in, 24, 25–29; as process, 34–35, 48; projects for creative, 119–127; reading out loud, 62–63; recognizing good, 49–53, 64–66; removing writer's block, 77; resources and readings on, 148; review phase in, 32–33; revision phase of, 32–33; role in every course, x; sequencing assignments, 42–43; structuring assignments, x–xi, xv–xvi, 36–42; student-generated criteria for, 53; traditions of disciplinary, 1–3; ways to promote, 130–137; on writing, 98–99. *See also* Low-stakes writing; Reviews; Revisions; *and specific writing approaches*

Writing across curriculum (WAC): advocating, 143–144; challenges implementing, 11–18; defined, xix, 2; effectiveness of, 139; formal programs in, 5–6; history of programs in, 3–6; modeling for colleagues, 142–143; overcoming faculty resistance to, 12–14; re-inventing assignments for, xvi–xvii, 7–11; readings and resources, 18–19, 131–132, 148–149; student resistance to, 14, 17–18

"Writing Across the Curriculum" (Maimon), 18

Writing Centers Association Conferences, 132

Writing (Cowan and Cowan), 27

Writing in the Academic Disciplines, 1870–1990 (Russell), 18

Writing in the disciplines (WID): defined, xix, 2–3; effectiveness of, 139; student benefits for, 7–9

Writing Program Administrators Conferences, 132

Writing-to-learn (WTL): benefits of, 16; defined, xix, 3; doubting and believing game, 80–82; effectiveness of, 139; scope of in quantitative disciplines, 9–11; student-authored textbooks, xvii, 110–113; three-minute themes, 82–84. *See also* Low-stakes writing

Writing Without Teachers (Elbow), 26

Written Communication, 131

Y

You Make the Call exercise, 66

Z

Zobel, J., 50